"People of substance know their purpose—their reason for being. Their careers and businesses are mirrored reflections of who they are and why they exist. *The On-Purpose Business* is masterfully written to help you identify the purpose of your enterprise, giving it meaning and divine guidance."

John Kalench, founder and president,
Millionaires In Motion, Inc.

"*The On-Purpose Business* is a message every business leader needs to read. I loved the story and the profound message spoken through the voice of the characters. This book holds the true essence of leadership."

Elizabeth Jeffries, CSP, CPAE,
partner, Tweed Jeffries, LLC

"*The On-Purpose Business* makes perfect sense. This extraordinary book provokes deep thinking and offers hope that your life and work can definitely reflect your inner purpose."

Gary O'Malley,
O'Malley Associates

"Purpose, vision, and mission are the driving forces of the successful company of the future. *The On-Purpose Business* is a great tool to help you find your way."

Patrick Kelly, CEO,
PSS/World Medical, Inc.

"*The On-Purpose Business* is a powerful paradox. It's about business, yet deeply personal. It opens a wide vista on leadership, yet sharpens a leader's focus. The message is about 'what's' and 'how's,' yet examines why they're meaningless without a compelling 'why.'" It both challenges and comforts. This is a timeless book."

Bob Mueller, sales development manager,
American Suzuki Motor Corporation

# The
# ON-PURPOSE
# BUSINESS

A MODERN PARABLE

# The
# ON-PURPOSE
# BUSINESS

## DOING MORE OF
## WHAT YOU DO BEST
## MORE PROFITABLY

KEVIN W. MCCARTHY

PIÑON PRESS

P.O. BOX 35007, COLORADO SPRINGS, CO 80935

## OUR GUARANTEE TO YOU

We believe so strongly in the message of our books that we are making this quality guarantee to you. If for any reason you are disappointed with the content of this book, return the title page to us with your name and address and we will refund to you the list price of the book. To help us serve you better, please briefly describe why you were disappointed. Mail your refund request to: PiñonPress, P.O. Box 35002, Colorado Springs, CO 80935.

Library of Congress Catalog Card Number: 97-41103
ISBN 1-57683-321-6

Cover design: Marcy Shultz
Cover illustration: Dan Jamison

Some of the anecdotal illustrations in this book are true to life
and are included with the permission of the persons involved.
All other illustrations are composites of real situations, and any
resemblance to people living or dead is coincidental.

McCarthy, Kevin W.
    The on-purpose business : doing more of
what you do best more profitably / Kevin McCarthy
        p. cm.
    ISBN 1-57683-321-6
    1. Management by objectives. 2. Strategic
planning. 3. Leadership. I. Title.
HD30.65.M377 1998
658.4'012—dc21                97-41103
                                    CIP

Printed in the United States of America

2 3 4 5 6 7 8 9 10 / 06 05 04 03

# CONTENTS

*To Judith.*
*With this book,*
*Thanks for your encouragement, vision, and belief in*
*seeing it through.*
*For everything else,*
*Thanks for putting your flag in my ship and setting*
*sail together.*

# FOREWORD

KEVIN MCCARTHY's first book, *The On-Purpose Person*, was a birthday present. I read the book on a business trip and was so taken by it that I called Kevin. We connected and I invited him to my offices on his next trip to California. We became instant friends and admirers of each other's work.

As a vociferous reader of books, with over 30 years of reading or browsing six to ten books per week, I've read more than 10,000 books. *The On-Purpose Person* is one of my top five favorites. Kevin's first book changes lives; *The On-Purpose Business* can change the world. These books deserve—no, need—to be best-sellers. Both embrace timeless messages that the world needs right here and right now.

*The On-Purpose Business* teaches you to get on-purpose, stay on-purpose, and attract the right people—all to accomplish more than you could hope and aspire to achieve alone. What could be more important?

Don't let the quick read deceive you. *The On-Purpose Business* has substance for the soul. This brilliant parable engages, educates, and entertains all in about the time it takes to see a movie. Few people communicate so much in so few words. Kevin shares with my departed friend, Og Mandino, the gift of presenting profound messages in memorable stories that everyone will read, re-read, share, remember, and tell again and again.

*The On-Purpose Business* works at many levels. With a quick reading, you'll end any confusion about the difference between purpose, vision, and mission statements.

You'll also learn about The Four Pillars of an on-purpose business: The Purpose Principle, Think Inc!, The Service Model, and The Manner. There's more in this book—much, much more.

The genius of the book lies below the surface, that by using these pillars you'll excel. If you earn a paycheck, then you run a business called your career. If you own or run a business, then you know the challenges. Read this book and learn to manage *your* career, future, and business to become more successful than you ever dreamed.

The explosion of telecommuting, home-based businesses, and outsourcing in combination with the deepening spiritual awareness signal the desire for meaningful work as a way of life. Purpose and meaning matter. Kevin gives us a glimpse into the coming age of purpose and meaning. We have information overload and need to connect it into wisdom; this book does just that.

We may one day look back from the third millennium and see that The On-Purpose Business was the seminal work at the heart of an unmatched business revival—one that restored business as a high and noble calling of service to God, self, family, country, and our world.

With all that said, just read it! You'll love the story.

MARK VICTOR HANSEN
Co-author, New York Times #1 best-selling
*Chicken Soup for the Soul* series

# PREFACE

My hope for you is that the message of *The On-Purpose Business* inspires you. I highly recommend you first read this parable for enjoyment and the moral of the story. Having taken in the story, next go back with your highlighter and pen in hand. Dig into the details of the models and the four pillars to find what's most applicable to you.

Don't let the brevity of the book fool you. Perhaps you've heard the expression, I didn't have time to write you a short letter, so I wrote you a long one instead. The original manuscript of *The On-Purpose Business* was double the size of the book in your hands. I needed four years and three extensive re-writes to painstakingly distill it to this essence. There are sentences that could be the basis of entire books. Do you understand why I encourage multiple reading of the book? This is highly concentrated.

The original concept of the on-purpose business was developed ten years ago and has been field-tested ever since in my businesses and those of consulting clients. These essentials are packed into a story to involve you as much as possible. I hope you see yourself as the man, the main character in the story, regardless of your gender.

Be forewarned, there's a tension in the book between the man's job, career, and business. You may not perceive yourself as owning a business, yet you do! It's called your career and it's made up of a lifetime of jobs, projects or responsibilities. Managing a career shares all the same elements as managing a business. I hope you'll come to appreciate this perspective and the dynamic challenges it presents.

*The On-Purpose Business* is for busy people who want to take their job, career, business or life to a higher and more meaningful level of performance. Think of it as strategic thinking and positioning for the strategically impaired. If you're caught in the doing day-after-day and know that something just has to change, then you'll truly gain a significant payoff with this simple, systematic approach.

If you read my first book, *The On-Purpose Person*, you're probably curious about the relationship of these two titles. *The On-Purpose Business* stands on its own. It is kin to *The On-Purpose Person*. They share characters and style. In this second book you'll once again journey with the man, learn from some old mentors, and meet some new ones.

*The On-Purpose Business* advances the theme of being on-purpose into our lives where we join, belong, and contribute—organizations. We have a natural affinity for belonging. We belong to families and to places of work, worship, volunteer and play. All are organizations.

The setting for this book is a business. It could just as easily have been a hospital, school, non-profit organization, church or association. Based on the field testing in a variety of situations, I've found the concepts apply broadly even if the jargon differs in each setting; for example: customer becomes patient, guest, or member; sales becomes evangelism, admissions or membership; and profit becomes revenue, income or benefit.

When you finish reading *The On-Purpose Business*, I invite you to read *The On-Purpose Person*. Independently, each book holds a special message. Together, there's an intended synergism as I am writing from a larger plan of being on-purpose in all areas of our lives.

Your comments and questions are most welcomed. Your stories feed me. Please let me know how the book affects your life or how your organization is putting *The On-Purpose Business* into practice. My phone number and addresses are listed in the back of this book under On-Purpose Resources.

Be On-Purpose!

KEVIN W. MCCARTHY

# ACKNOWLEDGMENTS

It always amazes me to watch the movie credits roll and see all the people involved in making it. Similarly, I'm stunned reflecting on all the people who have left their imprint on this work. I'm humbled to realize so many people cared enough to give of themselves.

First, I must thank my family. My children, Charles and Anne, have watched me disappear into my home office for hours on end. I asked them not to disturb me. And as two kids under age seven, they honored my request almost as many times as they didn't. Oh, well! What delightful interruptions. My wife, Judith, helped make time for writing by managing schedules to accommodate those truly intense, yet flowing times of my writing. My parents and my brother, Bob, are loving and generous champions with my family and work. Without them, none of this would be possible. My mother-in-law, AKA Granny, opened Woodlawn for long family respites that provided extended and uninterrupted writing opportunities while I stayed home.

For his always forthright opinions and editing on the original manuscript, I hold Paul Crowell in highest esteem. What an example of a servant-friend! Paul, I'm passing along your example to others. Randy Robertson, Alan Skelton, Glenn Hettinger, Gary Hatter and Kirk Squires all gave detailed and honest feedback on the first (and lengthy) manuscript.

My clients have willingly provided an open acceptance for my on-purpose perspective. I'm especially appreciative of George Maynard and his team at Orlando Regional

Healthcare Foundation. Having a client in my hometown committed to making this dream a reality has been a blessing. More importantly, I value the friendship. To Susan Batchelor who ten years ago engaged me to teach an hour and a half presentation to a group of real estate brokers on strategic planning . . . little did we know what was begun.

Others of special note are: Steve Levee, Bruce Nygren, Murray Fisher, Bert Ghezzi, Jim Keeter, Mark Modesti, Greg Voisen, Jeff Tallman, Jay Brophy, my professors at The Darden School, the professors and mentors of The On-Purpose College, Mark Eldridge, Elsom Eldridge, Jr., Pam Dean, Karen Nichols, Marilu Hall, Monica Calzolari, Claire Carter, Chic Thompson, Dana Kyle, Laurie Hartman, Lisa Williams, Mark Kellum, Perry Nies, Hal and Trudy Williamson, Robert and Jamie Thomas, Jackie Wildermann, Tom Farr, Paul Chiampa, Charlie Stuart, John Smith, Don Curran, Dr. George Andreae, Faye Hobbs, Gordon Caswell, Terry Taylor, the team at Bob Smith's American ReproGraphics and especially Peggy, Hank Franklin, Joe Barnes, and John Rosenblum. Each in his or her own special way either opened doors for me or tried to kick me through one when I needed it.

Thank you to the men and women who wrote endorsements. You are kind to place the mantle of your good name and reputation upon this book. I especially want to thank Mark Victor Hansen for his foreword.

Many readers of *The On-Purpose Person* have called or written the office asking for *The On-Purpose Business.* These almost daily phone calls have been a true source of encouragement. Thank you.

Thank you to the publishing team at Piñon Press and NavPress. Dean Galiano is directly responsible for this book being where it belongs. Thanks, Dean, for your steadfast belief in the importance of being on-purpose. Thanks, Kent Wilson, for being open and willing for NavPress to be a publishing partner in this endeavor. Sue Geiman and Nanci McAllister fostered me through the transitions with skill and warmth. Lori Mitchell was the managing editor who skillfully managed this manuscript and even more skillfully managed me! The others in editing, design, sales and marketing, PR and operations—Thanks! I'm proud to be a small part of the NavPress and Navigator family.

Please forgive me if I failed to mention your name in thanks. It would only be an oversight, not . . . on-purpose.

Last but not least, I thank God for this awesome gift and message of being on-purpose. I am finally willing to be a faithful steward and bold professor of this message. When I am at my eleventh hour, I hope and pray that I soon will hear you say, "Well done, good and faithful servant; you have been faithful over a little, I will set you over much; enter into the joy of your Master."

# 1

# THE INTERVIEW

▼

*There are two fundamentally differing views of human nature and work. The "objective view" sees work as a source of economic means. The "subjective view" is concerned with the effects of work on the person. By the early twenty-first century, quality will become a commodity, and companies will be distinguished by the wholeness of their people.*

**Bill O'Brien**
*former CEO,
Hanover Insurance Company*

"**S**he's here," chirped Jackie, the man's assistant. "The receptionist just called. I'll greet her, okay?"

"Please. Let me gather my thoughts before the interview," responded the man.

"She" was a reporter from the *Wall Street Journal*. Two years ago an article in this newspaper had forecast the imminent demise of the company. Her arrival today signaled a broad recognition of a corporate turnaround nothing less than spectacular.

Anticipating her typical questions about his "secrets" on the renewal, he could only smile to himself. *Do I tell her a gold pocket watch made all the difference?* he wondered. Picking up the timepiece from its desk stand, he caressed it in his left palm and then wound it. The extraordinary workmanship, beauty, and jeweled mechanism made it an object of functional art, but more than its art or function set it apart.

This watch had a story. Opening the delicate gold locket cover and thumbing the inscription, he read, "To Frederick W. Taylor, in honor of forty-eight years of faithful service and leadership." He smiled in fond remembrance of his departed boss and influencer.

This watch served as a tangible remembrance of a man, his era and lifestyle; it was a symbol of the past, a reminder in the present, and a touchstone for the future. The ever-ticking watch reminded him of lessons learned in business and, importantly, in life.

His mind flashed to Fred Taylor's retirement party two years ago. . . .

▼ ▼ ▼

## THE OLD MAN'S WATCH

Fred's nickname was "the Old Man." His career had begun as a teenager in the mail room and ended forty-eight years later as the chief executive officer. Despite Fred's shortcomings, the man had to admire his lifetime accomplishments. With a firm hand on the helm, Fred Taylor was the company and the company was Fred.

Still, the man couldn't help thinking, *It's a good thing the Old Man's retiring. His heart attack provided a graceful early exit.* Undoubtedly, a healthy Fred would have been pressured by the board of directors to step aside. As Fred told it, he was "going out on top—a winner," but in almost everyone else's mind, the Old Man was self-deceived. The company was dangerously past due for a competitive overhaul—beginning at the top.

Business had changed, as had the times, and the Old Man had fought it. Navigating the shifting currents of the economy and the ever-quickening rapids of business overwhelmed Fred. "Gone are the good old days," he would lament. Clinging to old patterns and perspectives, Fred's methods were no longer relevant. He called it "sticking to fundamentals," except that the fundamentals had changed.

Years ago, under Fred's command, the company had fallen into a comfort zone, a subtle winner's arrogance. As the executives grew more content and self-satisfied, competition emerged. It was unimaginable that small start-ups could touch, let alone erode, the market leadership of the company.

Now they were struggling just to keep up. *It's like a champion prizefighter who stays in the ring one too many bouts*, thought the man. Momentum and reputation sustained the business and masked the real problems. The ultimate undoing wasn't going to be competition—it would be denial.

The stakes were high and the margin for error thin. Profits were being squeezed by rising expenses and falling prices. Cash was tight. Longtime customers were moving to smaller, faster, lower-priced producers. The priorities of the company and the employees were often at cross purposes. Turf battles between vice presidents were the norm. Quality was suffering.

It was a wonder that product got out the door, and when it did ship, defects or shipping mistakes were creating frequent and costly returns and remakes. The competitive edge was blunt, and customer complaints were soaring to new heights. Even their largest and best contract customer, the GEOMay Company, issued complaint after complaint.

Fred hadn't grasped the threat to the very existence of the business. Mired in the past, he ruled with a stubborn, tightfisted hold. A silent mutiny stirred. The vice presidents reported what he wanted to hear and did as they saw fit. Their intentions were positive, but the results were not. These deceitful "white lies" hamstrung the operation. This was a business divided against itself. The trickle of deceit eventually became a flood of ethical compromises. Truth was consigned a two-bit role in this business drama.

Fred's gold pocket watch symbolized the best of a bygone era that revered truth and values—a time when one's character and reputation clearly stood above the current quarterly earnings and personal fortune, a time when one's life was more than a job and collective status symbols.

The man knew a gold retirement watch was unlikely in his future. The global nature of business; the impact of technology, mergers, and changes in distribution; and the swings in consumer demands were a few of the factors bursting the once-secure cocoon of a career within a single company.

Fred began his farewell address, "Forty-eight years ago this past June, I joined this company. . . ." The man's thoughts drifted from the Old Man's retirement rhapsody to the enormous challenges that lay before him as the Old Man's replacement. To calm the whirlwind of confusing thoughts and emotions blowing through his mind, he needed help.

He knew just the person to call for help: his old friend, the professor. . . .

▼ ▼ ▼

THE MAN'S STORY

Jackie escorted the reporter into the man's office. After a few pleasantries, the interview began. "To what do you attribute the successful turnaround of this company?" she asked right on cue.

Holding the timepiece in his hand, the man began, "Do you see this gold pocket watch?"

# 2

# Purpose Is at the Heart

▼

*Effective leaders delegate a good many things; they have to or they drown in trivia. They do not delegate the one thing that only they can do with excellence, the one thing that will make a difference, the one thing that will set the standards, the one thing they want to be remembered for. They do it.*

**Peter F. Drucker**
*The Leader of the Future*

L eaning back in his chair, the professor sat staring out his office window. Unnoticed, the man entered the office and proclaimed, "Caught you! Daydreaming again."

Twirling to face the man, the professor laughed, stood up, and threw open his arms. The friends embraced. "I was on a two-minute vacation. It's a relaxation technique a colleague named Brophy taught me. He's compiled *Dr. Brophy's Guidebook of Two-Minute Vacations* that's filled with short games, getaways, and ideas to re-create. You caught me being on-purpose."

"As always," the man laughed.

The professor resumed, "So what's the purpose of your visit?"

The man and the professor had a history of trust, so the man immediately disclosed, "Briefly . . . I'm the new president of my company. It's in a shambles, and . . . I need help, now!"

"What's at stake?" asked the professor.

Pondering the question for a moment, the man answered, "The future of this company and the jobs of many people, including my own."

"Hm-m-m," the professor sighed as he scratched behind his right ear. "Step one, what's the purpose of your organization?"

The man replied, "We have a mission statement."

Wincing, the professor asked, "What's it say?"

The man stammered with embarrassment, "Huh? I, er, ah — I don't know."

The professor shook his head in disbelief. "Amazing! The president of the company doesn't know the *mission statement*! Call your office and have a copy faxed over here." The professor's eyes narrowed. "And it's a *purpose statement* not a mission statement. Get it right!"

"Pardon my mixup," the man said, feeling the professor's heat. He phoned Jackie to have her fax it.

The professor didn't buy the apology. "It's no mixup, it's lack of understanding. Don't casually interchange purpose with its offspring of vision and mission. They're not synonyms. The misuse of these rich words has significance at the very essence of life itself."

His curiosity piqued, the man asked, "Professor, what *is* the difference between purpose, vision, and mission? Obviously, I still don't get it."

In a measured voice and with a big grin, the professor announced, "I will joyfully explain the difference. I *live* to answer that question. First, there is only one purpose. But there are many visions—and several missions for each vision."

The man began taking notes in a journal.

The professor continued, "Next, we'll reference purpose, vision, mission, and values to your body."

"To my body?" inquired the man.

"Yes! The concepts become real and tangible this way. You need an On-Purpose Pal to help you remember.

"First, purpose is from the heart. Draw a heart in the middle of your paper and label it 'Purpose.'" The man did it.

"Purpose resides in the heart," the professor said. "The ancient Greeks said the heart is where mind, body, and soul converge. I buy that. Purpose envelops love. So be in touch with your heart," he said while touching his own heart with the fingertips of his right hand.

The professor continued his lesson. "Next is vision. Draw a head with two eyes above the heart. Label it 'Vision.'"

"Vision resides in your mind's eye. It is your dreams and possibilities.

"Close your eyes." The man did as he was told. "Now imagine a blue elephant. . . . Its tusks are green . . . and its toenails are painted hot pink . . . and it's wearing purple boxer shorts with yellow polka dots. Do you see it?"

The man burst into laughter. "What a sight!"

"That's your mind's eye. Now, with your eyes still closed, imagine your business in its ultimate vision or potential. Dream in rich detail." While pacing meditatively, the professor engaged the man's imagination. "Who are your customers and why? How are they served? What processes and plans are in place to ensure successful service? How's it feel walking around your business?

"See your annual report. What do the sales and profit charts look like? How's your teamwork?

"Think about the people working there — are they smiling, happy . . . enthusiastic, confident . . . excited and purposeful?

"How does the organization give back to the community?

"What do you do on a day-to-day basis?"

The man sat with eyes closed and a smile from ear to ear. Finally he said, "This is terrific."

"And it all resides where?"

"In my imagination, or my mind's eye as you describe it," the man answered.

"Yes. Your vision and purpose need to be connected and aligned.

"Here's a warning: A vision not anchored in your purpose is often just a costly distraction."

The man opened his eyes and resumed jotting notes. "You're right about visions without purpose," he said. "I've chased some dreams only to find they weren't mine." He prompted the professor. "Tell me about missions."

"Draw hands and feet on your On-Purpose Pal."

The professor continued, "Missions are what we do to fulfill the vision that is anchored in our purpose. Missions are the 'doing' aspects of our lives. Purpose is the being, and visions are the seeing."

"For the first time," said the man, "the difference between these words makes sense. They're not synonyms." Pressing on, he asked, "Where are our values reflected on the body?"

"Where do you think?" countered the professor.

"The heart?" the man guessed.

"Well, we already said the heart contains our purpose. Want a clue?" he offered. The man nodded compliantly. "If you violate your values, where will you feel it?"

The man remarked, "In my gut. You know, the expression 'My gut tells me something's not right about this.' Right?"

"Yes, your gut! The other place for values is your throat. It's the gatekeeper to outer temptations. In other words, if a vendor attempts an illegal kickback in exchange for a contract, you would have a choking or a gag response. Your values are warning you not to mistakenly ingest the indecent proposal. Otherwise, you live with the compromise in your gut. Violate your values frequently, and it's called an ulcer.

"Back to your drawing. Put a small circle at the throat and a big oval at the belly to symbolize values on your body."

"I like it," the man said. "I can remember that."

The professor posed the question, "What's the worst violation of one's values?"

"Being off-purpose?" the man guessed.

"Yes! Being off-purpose is the ultimate separation and loss of integrity. It leaves one with an empty feeling. When we're off-purpose, we're more easily tempted by artificial fulfillment instead of the pure nourishment of purpose. Some people indulge in drugs and alcohol, food, sex, work, shame, or other destructive behaviors. Hopelessness has a foothold."

The man winced. "Wow! That's intense. I've faced a few of those monsters myself."

"Align your purpose, visions, and missions. Another way of saying it is, when we've aligned our heart, head, and hands with our values, then we're living with integrity. It's called being on-purpose."

The professor continued, "As the leader in your business, you must be a person of high integrity because you set the standards. If you want the business to be on-purpose, you must personally be on-purpose.

"And everyone is a leader. Whether you're the company president or a mail room clerk, you bring your purpose to the position."

The professor stopped to look at his watch. "I'm teaching a class in ten minutes," he said with a start. "I need to run, so I'll give you an overview.

"Purpose builds on our past, lives in our present, and holds hope for our future. A purpose statement preamble begins with 'I exist to serve by. . . .' Therefore, purpose is the ultimate service concept.

"Now, consider your customer service programs and hiring in light of purpose. Purpose is our spiritual DNA from which our vision and missions sprout. From a divine perspective, purpose is God's will for your life. Purpose is infinite and eternal."

The man's eyes opened widely.

"Purpose is spiritual electricity," the professor continued. "Like electricity, it has been around since the beginning of time. But only after Benjamin Franklin identified and named electricity did people harness its awesome power. Edison's light bulb, Bell's telephone, the computer, television, and all the other electronic devices emerged thanks to one man, a kite, and a key.

"We're in our infancy when it comes to understanding and harnessing the power of purpose. Imagine the possibilities in our lives and society as our understanding and use of purpose mature. Recall that this," the professor said as he pointed to a poster of a light switch, "is the symbol of the on-purpose person. It reminds us to stay connected with our spiritual energy and turn it on."

"I like the analogy," the man offered. "Go on, please."

"Vision answers the question, 'Where are we going?' It is our hope; it inspires us today. It resides in our mind's eye or imagination. This future destination is a dream snapshot. We have an overall vision for our life and visions for each of the life accounts — spiritual, intellectual, physical, family, vocational, financial, and social. Vision is seeing our future.

"Missions are our doings in the present, right now, today. They are the current means and actions at hand. Missions focus on outward actions and address the question, 'What do we need to be doing today to fulfill and express our purpose and advance us toward our vision?' Missions are measurable, finite, and composed of specific goals with definite beginnings and endings.

"Values are learned and revealed internal governors of right and wrong that we feel in our gut and throat. Values are timeless regulators of our purpose in the world about us. They help us choose what is most important."

The fax machine in the professor's office buzzed and began coughing out the statement from the man's company.

# 3

# THE PURPOSE STATEMENT

▼

*"My job is in line with the president's job—to keep people happy."*

**John Wiggins**
*1995 Ruffies Trash Bags*
*National Sanitation Worker of the Year*

The professor read aloud from the man's paper: "Our mission is to pursue excellence by profitably serving our customers and adding value through quality products and services as the national leader in our industry while delivering a high rate of return to our stockholders."

The man was embarrassed. "That's the ultimate gag-on-it mission statement," he blurted. "It sounds like we bought a book of catchy business phrases and combined a bunch of 'em. Nine months of meetings and tens of thousands of dollars to write that! It lacks personality, punch, and heart."

The professor burst into laughter. "Well said! No wonder you couldn't remember it. Wad it into a ball and trash it."

The man obeyed. Then he asked, "What do I do next?"

"Turning around the company starts with a purpose statement and alignment with it. This includes your plan, people, process and performance for your customers, shareholders and community."

"You're right. We've been adrift without one. Professor, what is a purpose statement?"

The professor explained, "A purpose statement is simply two power-packed words that hone in on the constant uniqueness of the person or organization. It answers the question, 'Why do I exist?' The preamble begins with 'I exist to serve by . . .' and ends with two words."

"Two words—that's it?" the man asked.

"That's it. I told you purpose is spiritual DNA. Think of the two words as the X and Y chromosomes. Here are actual examples of purpose statements. *I exist to serve by . . . Setting Free; Celebrating Nature; Igniting Dignity; Inspiring Insight*; and *Liberating Greatness*. From these seeds individuals and organizations have grown and prospered, on-purpose!"

The man observed, "All the X chromosome words end with *-ing*, don't they?"

"Yes. That shows we're never finished being on-purpose. Remember, our purpose is eternal—in our past, present, and future. It isn't a single defining event; it's expressed and refined over one's lifetime."

"What about the second word, Professor? What's its role?"

"The second half of the purpose statement is the object of the activity. It brings focus and depth."

The man started to stand up. "Professor, I've got it. Thanks! How will I ever repay you?"

"Not so fast with the adieu," said the professor. "You came here because your business is in a shambles, remember?"

"That's right."

The professor looked the man dead in the eyes and said, "You need help. A purpose statement is a start, not a finish. What you want is an On-Purpose Business. You need a businessperson to help you. Let me reacquaint you with . . ."

"Bob Scott!" exclaimed the man as he snapped his fingers. The professor nodded his agreement. "Why didn't I think of him before? Back when I first met Bob, I told him I noticed he had a high-performance team at his company.

"Bob said, 'Thank you. We're an On-Purpose Business.'

"'What do you mean by that?' I asked.

"'We're very clear about the purpose of our company. We encourage each person to become an On-Purpose Person. We don't try to change people; we only want them to become more aware of their potential. It's a powerful and fulfilling linkage when the purpose of the person is aligned with the purpose of the organization.'

"Professor, I asked him how to develop an On-Purpose Business. Bob waved me off and said, 'Let's hold that conversation until another day.' In so many words he said my first priority was personal clarity around my purpose, and after that, we could address the needs of my organization."

"Your path is before you," encouraged the professor.

The professor and the man gave each other a hug. Then the professor went off to his class, while the man headed to his office to call Bob Scott and arrange a meeting.

# 4

# THE THREE PERSPECTIVES

▼

*When our first parents were driven out of Paradise, Adam remarked to Eve, "My dear, we live in an age of transition."*

**W. R. Inge (1860–1954)**
*Dean, St. Paul's Church, London*

Resting comfortably in a large upholstered chair, the man soaked in the ambience of Bob Scott's office. The warm setting of traditional furnishings and hardwood floors covered with oriental carpets reflected the person. Hunter green walls held magnificent oil paintings, charcoals, and etchings of presidents and landscapes. Contrasting this motif was a gleaming computer and communication system on Bob's desk.

They chatted until the man directed the conversation. "Please tell me about the On-Purpose Business."

"Let's get started," agreed Bob. "We'll begin with the three perspectives. The first is our place in the stream of history. The second is the organization relative to society. And the third is the interrelationship of the person, the business, and the society. These three perspectives are the backdrop of clues and patterns that help us anticipate the path ahead."

"So we can plan accordingly?" asked the man.

"Yes," Bob said. "First, let's look at our place in history. We live in the Knowledge Age, which advanced from the Industrial Age, which grew from the Farm Age, which was produced from the Stone Age. Right?"

"Right," agreed the man.

"What is the age beyond this present age?"

"I'm having enough trouble figuring out this present age," quipped the man. "What's the answer?"

"Not so fast," said Bob coyly. "Think this through. Here's a hint. Look at the relationship of technology and work. Through the ages we've risen from being hunters and gatherers to farmers to industrial workers to knowledge workers. How has the nature of our day-to-day work changed?"

The man's eyes lit up. "We've shifted from the work of

our hands to the work of our heads."

"And what's the next logical progression?" prodded Bob. The man deliberated further. He snapped his fingers as he was prone to do when he realized something. "It's like the On-Purpose Pal! We're going from our hands to our heads to our hearts."

"Right," Bob affirmed. "Paradoxically, in the midst of a seemingly chaotic and meaningless world, our society is speeding to the Age of Purpose. As our knowledge grows, we realize even more of what we don't understand. More knowledge will never be the answer. Meaning in life is an inner quality of which the mind is but a conduit."

"So how do I apply this perspective today?"

Bob answered, "Perspective number two is organizational perspective. The way to the right answers is to ask the right questions. What are the advantages of this insight? How might your company operate in the coming Age of Purpose? How can extraordinary people be attracted to work in this future age? What will be the nature of business? Will work support the family or the family support work? Can work become a place where the average person makes a positive difference in society?

"The On-Purpose Business has solutions to these questions," Bob continued. "The bottom line is that forward-thinking organizations offering meaningful opportunity will hold a strategic advantage over those that don't."

"I need it now," the man confessed.

"No, you don't," Bob corrected. "Strategic advantage is not the point at all. This isn't about competition, it's about the collaboration of persons and organization doing more of what they do best more profitably."

"This *is* different," the man remarked. "And the third perspective is . . . ?"

"Your personal perspective is the most important because you control it. Your viewpoint is your rudder to navigate the shifting currents of society and business.

"Along this line," Bob challenged, "why did you wait so long to come see me about the On-Purpose Business?"

"I was appointed president by the board only a few months ago. With Fred Taylor still there, the transfer of responsibility didn't come until recently."

Bob pressed, "I'll rephrase the question. Why did you wait until you became president? You needed to be in this process long before now."

"It wasn't as critical as it is now," said the man, cringing even as the words left his mouth.

"Excuses," Bob declared. "Responsibility follows preparedness. Are you prepared to lead?"

Bull's-eye! What a startling realization. Inside a few minutes Bob had nailed the man's darkest doubt. Was he adequate to fulfill his long-held dream of being president and CEO?

Thankfully, Bob was here to help him not hammer him. "You're right," the man admitted. "It's scary being responsible for a business. This is virgin territory for me. I need your help because I lack . . . a president's perspective and experience."

Bob comforted him by saying, "And the On-Purpose Business yields perspective but not experience. Experience you'll need to gain on your own."

The man asked, "Does anyone understand this brave new world of technology and change?"

"Yes, but their understanding isn't like what you're thinking. I'm talking about the business of business—what it means to run an organization, large or small. There are universal patterns to building an organization.

Learn these, use these, and you'll have highly transferable organizational intelligence."

"What patterns?" queried the man.

"They're the Four Pillars of the On-Purpose Business. They'll help you align and integrate the heart, head, and hands in service to God, self, and others."

"It sounds too simple," the man remarked.

"It is so plain that on day one in our orientation program we introduce the Four Pillars, Executives, department heads, mailroom clerks, receptionists, salespeople—everyone knows and uses them. We're all doing business alike. That makes the business of my business uncomplicated. I like that."

"You're committed to this, aren't you?" the man observed.

"Totally," Bob declared. "The Four Pillars will transform your business. The members of your team will see the company, their jobs, and their lives from a president's perspective. Your team members will rise to new heights of fun, performance, and reward."

"Can something this simple be that potent?"

"Don't make that mistake. Is complexity a benefit?"

"I guess not," conceded the man.

"I have another question for you, Bob. Why? Why are you helping me learn this?"

Bob laughed. "I'm helping me . . . you . . . and this community. This is the collaboration I spoke of earlier. Sharing this is on-purpose for me. I'm honored and privileged to do it.

"But there's one condition," Bob added. "Promise me that when the time is right, you'll do the same for another person. As I am your On-Purpose Partner, will you, too, freely share the Four Pillars?"

The man nodded.

"Great," Bob said. "Let's toast this occasion with a juice from The Club." They rose from their chairs and walked to The Club, a restaurant adjoining the R. D. Scott Company offices. "I'll give you an overview of the Four Pillars now that you know the three perspectives of history, interrelationships, and self."

# 5

# THE FOUR PILLARS

▼

*This company has the brain
of a for-profit and the soul
of a not-for-profit.*

**Rebecca Maddox**
*Inc. Your Dreams*

Afriendly hostess at The Club seated Bob and the man at a window overlooking the tranquil downtown park. A waiter promptly greeted them.

"Good morning, gentlemen. Hi, Bob!" He then turned to the man. "Welcome to The Club, sir."

"Good morning, Dave," Bob returned. "I'll have a glass of your fresh-squeezed Florida orange juice, please."

"Same for me," said the man.

"Right away, gentlemen." Dave headed to the kitchen.

Bob Scott explained, "Each of the Four Pillars is associated with a word beginning with the letter *M*. They are the Meaning, Mindset, Method, and Manner, respectively.

"Here's a quick overview." Borrowing the man's journal he numbered and labeled each corner of the page, 1, 2, 3, and 4.

With his pen point resting in the upper left corner, he began, "Pillar One—the Meaning is the heart of it, or the Purpose Principle. This describes the purpose of the person aligning with the purpose of the organization. We'll discuss Pillar One in a little bit."

Moving the pen to the upper right corner, Bob explained, "Pillar Two is the Mindset: *Think Inc!* This is an abbreviation for Think Incorporated. It means we need to be, think, and act as the president of our own company. The exclamation point creates an encouraging affirmation. I'm 'Bob, Inc!' Your assistant is 'Jackie, Inc!' Understand?"

"Yes," said the man. Rubbing his chin, he admitted, "I haven't been doing *Think Inc!*"

"It's not easy, but it can be learned." Bob added, "Each of us *is* a business of one. Commissioned salespeople and small business owners are acutely aware of this reality. Yet, the concept applies equally well to salaried and hourly people. They simply contract their services with one customer — their employer.

"Instilling and supporting the *Think Inc!* mindset regardless of our position, experience, or compensation is a profound mind shift. Most people aren't used to thinking as though they have a profit-and-loss responsibility. High personal responsibility and consequences are part of the deal.

"You'll soon meet Frances Allwood, a real estate broker, former team member, and friend. She'll share her story of *Think Inc!*"

The man gravitated to *Think Inc!* This was the mindset he needed. *Do I have this*? he wondered.

"Pillar Three is the Service Model, the Method of building any organization," Bob resumed, indicating the lower left corner of the paper. "Through Hal Trudy, my mentor and first On-Purpose Partner, you will be . . . shall we say, cultivated for your new role. Hal led a highly successful and profitable company prior to his retirement. The people in Hal's company learned and applied the Four Pillars. His business was highly valued because of the quality of its people. They're TOP Performers. By the way," Bob said, "TOP is an acronym for 'The On-Purpose.' Therefore, 'TOP Performer' means The On-Purpose Performer.

"Hal retired from his business a wealthy man in many ways. The transition for the next CEO was seamless — in contrast to your transition. Hal Trudy is an extraordinary man."

"I definitely look forward to meeting him," remarked the man. "Now, what about Pillar Four?"

In a measured voice Bob revealed, "Pillar Four — the Manner is about conducting one's business. That is a profound statement whether you realize it or not. This is why I urge you to take a paced approach to redeveloping your company. Business is a marathon, not a sprint. Altering the culture in your organization takes time rather than one swift pass of a laser-printed edict. It's one person, one heart, one head, and one pair of hands at a time."

The man asked, "Okay, what's the Manner?"

"The Manner is," Bob stated, "doing more of what you do best more profitably."

"Doing more of . . . what I do best . . . more profitably," the man repeated softly and slowly. "Doing more of . . . what I do best . . . more profitably." Rolling the words in his mind, he finally snapped his fingers in recognition. "Yes, I would love to do more of what I do best more profitably. That would be fun!" he proclaimed.

Now briefed on the Four Pillars, the man immediately began trying to make sense of it. "So building an On-Purpose Business is a matter of understanding and using the Four Pillars?"

"One closing comment," Bob inserted. "This begins with you. Be patient with the business for a time. You have to become a product of the Pillars yourself. Then you can begin to share them and duplicate them throughout your organization."

"So an On-Purpose Business is really a community," assessed the man, "with this common means of interacting and organizing. Fewer issues get in the way of progress and business."

"Exactly," acknowledged Bob.

"Wow!" exclaimed the man. "It never dawned on me that our greatest challenges are in the very organization of our business. Let's get started on Pillar One."

---
**6**
---

# PILLAR ONE —
# THE PURPOSE PRINCIPLE

▼

*Step One: Establish constancy of
purpose at the macro and micro
level with the focus on the
customer.*

**W. Edwards Deming**
*"Fourteen Steps to Quality"*

**"P**illar One—the Meaning embodies the Purpose Principle," Bob Scott began. "It is represented with the following diagram." Bob began drawing in the man's journal.

## The Purpose Principle™

$$Pp \Leftrightarrow Po$$

"Read this as 'The purpose of the person (Pp) aligned with the purpose of the organization (Po),'" Bob explained. "The Purpose Principle depicts the presence and alignment of two states: significance and belonging. These are two powerful needs people have. High alignment results in feelings of meaningful contribution. In other words, being on-purpose.

"Like Einstein's theory of relativity, $E=MC^2$, this depiction distills several complex concepts into something elegantly useful.

"The Purpose Principle is the only meaningful linkage between a person and an organization. A person and the legal entity, called a business in your case, have no natural affinity except a common purpose, the binding of the collective spirit of its people. A paycheck without purpose is just a mercenary's fee—an empty exchange for a task."

The man countered, "But my old boss, Fred Taylor, used to say, 'You need to separate your personal life from your business life.' This runs counter to conventional wisdom."

"Yes, it does," Bob unapologetically answered. "That Industrial Age mentality is as obsolete as the typewriter. A harsh separation of one's business and personal life isn't effective anymore. Our vocation can be a meaningful and integrated expression of our purpose. We need to be whole."

The man brushed the last remark aside with "That's idealistic."

"So, what's your ideal instead?" countered Bob.

"Work is work, and that's the way it is."

"That's not an ideal. That's a resignation to mediocrity." Resting his head on his right hand, the man agreed. "You're right. Please keep talking."

"Work as an expression of your purpose will become apparent in due course," comforted Bob. "Find opportunities that you can believe in with all your heart, and you'll succeed. Ignore the Purpose Principle and you're ultimately a shell of a person, conforming to ever-tightening systems and structures that try to induce desired behaviors from you.

"Motivation is from within. Tap it within yourself and you'll know how to help others do the same. Everyone wins."

"That's high alignment, right?" the man said.

"Exactly," Bob answered and then added, "low-alignment people are easy to spot. They stay unhappy in jobs for years or even longer until retirement just for the paycheck. They don't understand that life is too precious to sell out for a few dollars.

"The subtle yet costly killer of morale, quality, and profits is low alignment. Low-alignment people are often labeled as having a bad attitude. In fact, it's fear and the absence of faith that defines their life and situation."

The man nodded his head in total agreement. Bob pressed on. "Now imagine someone who believes life is meaningless. Alignment isn't possible because he or she brings no sense of purpose into the relationship. What you want are men and women who seek to make a difference with their lives. In the final analysis, one's heart"—Bob placed his fist over his heart—"has to be in anything to excel—a marriage, a job, a relationship, anything."

The man picked up on the comment. "I can see high alignment by the way a person's eyes light up, or by his or her body language and energy."

"Yes, yes," Bob agreed. "Imagine a workplace where people have that gleam of purpose in their eye, that bounce in their step. Purpose matters because purpose is a matter of the heart. I can't say that enough." Bob repeatedly tapped at the Purpose Principle in the man's journal to make his point. "This pillar is the heart and soul of an On-Purpose Business."

"When I walk into your business, I sense that," the man observed.

"Thank you! That's a high compliment."

Then Bob pressed on. "Have you ever heard someone say, 'I want to make a difference' or 'I want to know that my life matters?'"

"Sure, all the time."

"That's an inborn desire for the Purpose Principle."

The man snapped his fingers. "Yes! That makes sense. As leaders we have an enormous responsibility to articulate the purpose of the organization. Right?"

"Absolutely. Articulating and communicating the purpose of the organization is pivotal to our performance as chief executive officers. A clear and succinctly stated purpose attracts and helps retain the right people."

The man agreed. "People with their hearts in their work self-manage, connect with the work, and care that it's right. They're the best quality control available. It's not policies, it's an authentic desire to contribute, it's alignment. They have a strong reason why they're doing what they do. They have a 'good attitude.'"

With a sudden shift in countenance, the man covered his eyes with his right hand and began a troubled massage of his temples with his thumb and index finger. "I just realized something," he moaned. "Without a strong 'organizational why,' everyone creates his or her own 'why.' All those well-intended 'whys' ultimately come at cross-purposes. It's utter chaos. It's my company."

"This," Bob said as he pointed with his pen repeatedly to the drawing of the Purpose Principle, "is the most powerful concept and tool you'll ever learn about nourishing people and fashioning a sustainable and healthy organization. Pillar One is a must if your business is to be a TOP Performer, period."

The man's eyes lit up. "I see it. Now how do I use it?"

Bob laughed. "Great question! You'll use it everywhere and all the time. You'll use the Purpose Principle when you hire; when you target customer segments; when you engage a vendor; when you do strategic planning; when you develop a new program, such as a marketing or sales program; even in your accounting and information systems. When you forge a strategic alliance or merger, you'll be looking at your potential partner in terms of alignment. You'll use it in your day-to-day activities such as writing a letter, making a phone call, or scheduling your appointments. With insight it becomes obvious and inescapable, a second nature."

"Help me make this real in my business," the man said.

"No problem." Bob smiled. "You need to know about the On-Purpose Quadrant."

---

**7**

---

# THE ON-PURPOSE QUADRANT

▼

*To have a path of knowledge, a path with a heart, makes for a joyful journey…and is the only conceivable way to live. We must then think carefully about our paths before we set out on them, for by the time a person discovers that his path "has no heart," the path is ready to kill him. At that point few of us have the courage to abandon the path, lethal as it may be, because we have invested so much in it, and to choose a new path seems so dangerous, even irresponsible. And so we continue dutifully, if joylessly, along.*

**Carlos Castenada**
*The Fire from Within*

B ob flipped to a new page in the man's journal. "The On-Purpose Quadrant depicts the relationship of two alignments." He drew a large rectangle and divided it into four boxes. Holding up two fingers on his right hand, he began, "The two types of alignment are Technical and Tingle."

Down the left side he wrote *TECHNICAL*. "Technical alignment is the knowledge, experience, and talent needed in a job, process, or business. It's the ability to get the job done."

"And what in the world is Tingle?!" prompted the man.

Writing *TINGLE* at the bottom center, Bob continued, "Tingle is a . . . well . . ."—he struggled for words—"Tingle is a feeling, an inner desire to excel, to achieve high satisfaction. Perhaps you're head over heels in love; you're having the time of your life with goose bumps of excitement. You feel great about what you're doing, where you're headed, and who you are. That's High Tingle."

"Tingle!" The man chuckled as he said, "You and the professor keep things so real, so . . . user-friendly."

"C'mon, life's tough enough," Bob offered. "Why mess it up with unneeded complexity? Have some fun. Tingle *does* describe the feeling."

"You're right," the man conceded. "I never thought of Tingle in my work. Maybe that's my problem, I don't expect any Tingle."

Bob elaborated. "High-Tingle people use words like *calling, belief, intuition, desire, giftedness, destiny,* and *passion.* We talk in terms of coming from the heart. We're positive, hope-filled people."

Bob moved to the journal again. "This model integrates Technical and Tingle. It helps us apply the Purpose Principle." He filled in the quadrants:

## TOP Quadrant

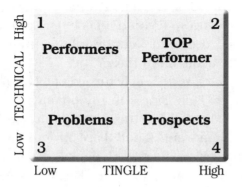

Pointing with his pen to the matrix, Bob said, "Let's pretend you want to hire the best possible people. From which quadrant do you select your candidates?"

"No doubt, Quadrant 2, TOP Performers."

"Why?" Bob asked.

"They're the High-Technical and High-Tingle people — the complete package. They're fully aligned with the purpose of the organization. They can do the job and are highly satisfied."

"Exactly," Bob agreed. "You'll never hire anyone the same way again as a result of TOP Quadrant. Whenever you hear 'TOP Performer,' think of a person with High-Technical *and* High-Tingle alignment.

"They are the people to hire, period. Avoid Problems. Relentlessly search for TOP Performers and Prospects.

"Most of us inadvertently bias our hiring process toward Performers because the Technical is a more obvious need. It's an incomplete search, however, more from ignorance than intention."

The man sat thinking, *This is so apparent. Yet, until now, I'd never thought or heard of it. "Tingle" puts into a word the feeling I have when I walk into the R. D. Scott Company. It's a High-Tingle workplace—an entirely different dimension on work and belonging.*

Bob sensed the man's contemplative manner and asked, "Are the lights on in there?"

"My light switch is definitely turned on. This makes so much sense. We lack Tingle in my business," the man confided. "Let's hear about the other quadrants."

Bob said, "Quadrants 2 and 3 are obvious. Quad 2, or TOP Performer, as we discussed, depicts the ideal candidates with High Technical and High Tingle. The Problems in Quad 3 have low capacity to perform the job and little heart for it. These candidates are a poor fit, period, and need to be elsewhere.

"Quads 1 and 4 are not so apparent. To explain these," Bob warned, "I'll use extreme lows and highs to make the point. But the fact is, most people are not at the extremes.

"In Quad 1 is the Performer—High Technical but Low Tingle. This person does the job, yet that's all it is—a task with performance standards to meet. There's little passion or belief. Performers often say, 'A bit of me dies every time I go to work.'"

"Hm-m-m," the man said.

Bob resumed, "In Quad 4 are Prospects, with High Tingle but Low Technical. These people are committed to the cause even if they can't significantly contribute to the effort—yet. With technical training, Prospects have the potential to become TOP Performers.

"There are two ways to develop TOP Performers:

"1. Help Performers find Tingle.

"2. Train Prospects with Technical.

"Prospects tend to be the richest, most consistent source of future TOP Performers, because Technical is generally learned more easily than Tingle can be instilled. High-Tingle people are valuable. We work hard to find and keep High-Tingle people. They're special. Tingle trumps Technical in our book.

"Ideally, we want both. Yet, Technical alignment ebbs and flows due to new technologies, market shifts, and a host of other factors that create obsolescence. High-Tingle people are valuable even when their Technical alignment momentarily falters, for whatever reasons. We keep High-Tingle people in our TOP Prospect Pool. It's a safe haven to transition Prospects into TOP Performers. Typically, Prospects quickly become TOP Performers again in another capacity."

The man chuckled as he said, "This sounds like competitive ice skating, where the competitors earn scores based on a combination of technical merit and artistic performance. The champion must excel in both to win."

"Exactly!" Bob affirmed. "Great analogy."

The man observed, "It occurs to me that there's a subtle yet profound distinction between the R. D. Scott Company and most businesses, including mine."

"What's that?" inquired Bob.

"In my business it isn't possible to have TOP Performers. We've failed to clearly articulate the purpose of our organization. That keeps us one-dimensional — Technical only. On the other hand, your business is built around both dimensions."

"Right," Bob answered. "I focus on integrating Technical and Tingle. Tingle without Technical is daydreaming. But still, my business absolutely must have Tingle."

"I agree," the man conceded. "Most of us who run businesses have built them around the Technical. We've missed the boat on Tingle."

Bob said, "Tingle is still obscure because the power of purpose is as yet unrealized. It keeps coming back to our heart." Again Bob placed his hand over his heart as he spoke. "In the business world especially, we don't speak much about the heart. In fact, it is foolishly put down, as are many things people don't understand."

The man defended the position. "Yes, but in the business world, coming from the heart implies an emotional and weak response. Business is logical and tough. That's just the way it is."

"Is it really?" Bob doubted. "On the contrary, coming from the heart or a place of purpose is absolutely the strongest place to be coming from. Changing someone's mind is easier than changing one's cause."

Bob continued, "Coming from the heart makes sense in life and in business. Long after the product or service is rendered, the feelings remain for the customer. Those feelings are the sense of alignment from both Technical and Tingle."

The man replied, "So the Purpose Principle is the touchy-feely stuff of business."

"Wrong," Bob corrected. "It is the very essence of business because businesses are ultimately people serving people. All the other stuff—the financial, marketing, legal, accounting, and so forth—are Technical processes supporting the path of purpose, the line of service. Tingle with customers, team members, or vendors is managed like any other resource.

"Because it's intangible, it's easy to overlook. But safe refuge in hard, cold numbers is folly. Ignore Tingle and you're managing to a third, maybe even a quarter, of the potential of the business in real terms."

"A third to a quarter of potential!" the man exclaimed.

"That's a bold statement. This is a new perspective for me. You know, 'Business is business.' That was one of Fred Taylor's favorite expressions."

"Yes, and 'All's fair in love and war,' right? Wrong! Please don't use those unfortunate clichés to justify unreasonable behaviors in the name of the holy grail of business. They're simply trite excuses for harmful and unhealthy behaviors that wring the Tingle out of us.

"In the Industrial Age, management got away with that attitude. That didn't make it right. People have always mattered."

The man was struck by Bob's certainty on these matters. But Bob was right. "Business is business" had never been a satisfactory response, only a condescending put-down implying, *If you don't know any better, I'm not explaining it to you.* In on-purpose terms, it was a lost teachable moment.

Because of his long association with the Old Man, the man found himself using Fred's expressions far too often at work and at home. Bob convicted him of his error. The Purpose Principle took root in his mind.

Bob Scott grinned. "Let's take a little break. May I treat you to one of our world-famous chocolate chip cookies hot out of the oven?"

"Absolutely," said the man.

Bob called Dave to their table and placed the order. A plate of cookies arrived with two tall ice-cold glasses of milk. The aroma was devastatingly delicious. With the man's first bite of cookie, a string of melted chocolate goo fell to his lower lip. He commented, "Um-mmm! These are great! Being off-purpose never tasted so good." Like two schoolkids at recess, they halted their purpose talk and chatted about their families and favorite sports teams.

---
**8**
---

# THE ON-PURPOSE PARADOX

▼

*Build the people, and the people
will build the business.*

Attributed to **Brownie Wise**
*Innovator of the Tupperware Home Party*

The chocolate chip cookies provided a needed break from their discussion of the On-Purpose Business.

Now the man had more questions. Probing onward, he said, "It seems that the *customer* should be the focus of the business, not the purpose or alignment. A business that gets too inwardly focused is destined for problems. Where's the customer in this?"

"You've been well-schooled in business," Bob commented and paused to choose his next words. The man delighted at the compliment until Bob added, "Except that customer focus alone falls short of the mark."

"I don't get it," the man admitted. "Everything I read says that customer focus is the be-all and end-all for a business."

"I understand. But it's still only a piece of the whole concept," Bob stated matter-of-factly.

"How so?"

"An On-Purpose Business is designed and dedicated to serving. Recall that purpose statements begin with 'I exist to serve by . . .' The on-purpose paradox is that in serving the customer, you also serve your organization, your greater community, yourself, and God. It's a complete and wholesome cycle of service. Everyone is a winner, or it's no deal."

"That's an unattainable standard," protested the man.

"Tell me then," countered Bob, "whom will you choose to deny serving? The customer? Your community? Your organization? Yourself? Your family? God?" He added a caution, "Think before you speak."

Pondering Bob's question and warning, he knew the answer. Bob was right. Still he protested, "It's a matter of semantics. It's all one and the same."

Bob firmly held his ground. "You've missed the point.

I've seen businesses so customer focused at the employees' expense that the employees were emotionally bankrupt. The customer is happy with the transaction, but the employee is trashed. How long do you think someone with options will stay on a job if day after day he's a customer doormat? Particularly if company policy dictates that 'the customer is always right.'"

The man acknowledged, "Not long, I imagine."

"Right. As a result, the company has high turnover, burnout problems, and high personnel costs for recruiting, training, and the like. In the end, customer service suffers because people are always worried about whether they'll have a job or not. The primary directive of customer service ultimately erodes and undermines a business. The business fails, so the community loses a resource. Crazy, isn't it?"

"Yes. Yet," the man persisted, "'the customer is always right' is a stalwart rule of thumb for doing business. How can you say it isn't right?"

"I simply said it misses the mark; it's incomplete. It has its place, yet it can't be unilaterally applied without serious negative consequences. The fact is, customers are sometimes wrong. When we have insight, we have an obligation to serve customers by sharing our insight and giving them the choice. Purpose is inclusive. The person serving is being served while serving another, which all serves a greater good. Think of it this way: TOP Businesses have TOP Customers."

"That makes good sense," the man replied. "Is it always possible to have high alignment?"

Bob laughed. "Of course not. That's why Pillar Four is 'Doing More of What You Do Best More Profitably.' This pillar is about seeking ultimate service opportunities. A question we frequently ask ourselves around here is, 'What is your ultimate TOP Opportunity?' Who are the customers? Why does serving them give you joy? Describe the service with words and pictures. What steps are needed? How does the customer respond? Clarifying one's TOP Opportunity is a powerful exercise." Bob added, "Pillar Three, the Service Model, will help you tremendously."

Just then, Dave, the waiter, came to the table with a cordless phone. "Bob, excuse me. It's your secretary, Helen, with a phone call for your guest."

Dave handed the phone to the man who released the hold button. "Hello!" He listened briefly, then said, "Thanks, Helen. Go ahead and transfer the call." After a moment, the man said, "Hi, Jackie. What's up?"

"Sorry to interrupt. Bad news," Jackie disclosed. "Fred Taylor was just rushed to the hospital from his home. Apparently, he's had another heart attack."

Excusing himself from Bob, the man took off for the hospital. As his car raced, so did his mind. His was in a love-hate relationship with Fred. In one way the Old Man was like a protective father to him, but in another way he had been like a neglectful and abusive father. He cared enough for Fred to be there for him, but on the other hand, he didn't understand why he was even bothering because Fred would have told him, "You can't afford to be making hospital calls on company time. Business is business."

The man gave a sad smile, thinking once again of Fred's motto. With Fred, the scorecard was always money. The man knew that money drives people only so far. Eventually they hit an impass. Being treated as a cog in the wheel is degrading.

*What a difficult way of doing business*, thought the man. His eyes were opening to the challenging circumstances he had been working under these past years. He had never known of other possibilities. He was learning that The On-Purpose Business is about service, openness, alignment, permanence, respect, and the heart.

Heart! That sparked a thought about Fred's heart as he pulled into the hospital garage. After parking the car he paused for a calming moment behind the wheel. Considering the Old Man's "heart condition," he thought, *What must be going through Fred's mind right now? As his life is passing before him, are there regrets, unfulfilled dreams, or peace?*

# 9

# PILLAR TWO — THE MINDSET

▼

*Now is the time to recognize . . .
that for every right there is a
corresponding obligation, for
every choice there is a
consequence.*

**Finola Bruton**
*wife of Ireland's Prime Minister John Bruton*

A week had passed since the man bolted to the hospital. Fred Taylor suffered a congestive heart failure. The man had visited with Mrs. Taylor, who was waiting in recovery. Unlike Fred, who had a strong, driven personality, Mrs. Taylor was a gracious woman with a quiet inner peace and strength. The man thought, *It must be true: opposites attract.*

Now the man was anxious to resume his On-Purpose Business lessons. Bob Scott had arranged two meetings for him, one with Frances Allwood and a second with Hal Trudy.

Frances Allwood's name was instantly recognizable because it was plastered on For Sale signs all over town. According to Bob, her mastery of Pillar Two — *Think Inc!*—had transformed her career.

Arriving promptly at Bob's office, he was introduced to Frances. His first impressions of her were that she showed high energy, self-confidence, and smarts. Her ebony skin was smooth and gave the impression of a much younger woman than her forty-five years. In the lapel of her nicely tailored suit she wore a gold pin with a light switch bearing the words "Be On-Purpose!"

"I like your lapel pin," the man remarked.

She responded with a laugh. "Thank you! You just reminded me to be on-purpose."

The man smiled. "That's pretty clever."

Frances explained, "Every outfit I own has an on-purpose pin on it. In my business—hold that, in my life—there are a b-i-l-l-i-o-n distractions," she dramatically stretched her arms for effect, "drawing me off-purpose. Thanks to these little pins, I have an army of On-Purpose Partners." She winked and added, "For free."

Bob Scott observed, "You two will get along great." He then asked the man, "How's Fred?"

"Fred's recovery will be slow, given the heart damage. Thanks for asking."

Turning to Frances, the man offered, "I'm excited to learn about Pillar Two."

Bob excused himself and offered them the use of his conference room. "I'll be back shortly," he said. Then to Frances, "He's seeing Hal Trudy after your visit."

Frances's face lit up. "What an opportunity! I listed and sold Hal's house when he retired. He's a true gardener—loves to get his hands dirty."

The two settled into chairs in Bob's conference room, and Frances asked, "What do you know about Pillar Two?"

"Bob talked about it once, but that was a while ago," the man answered. "Why don't you start over?"

"Great," said Frances. "Pillar Two is *Think Inc!* It means each person is the owner and president of his or her business. It means I manage to a profit or loss. It means I utilize and control certain resources for creating products and services. I create systems . . . manage the environment . . . lead when needed . . . get out of the way when I'm not needed . . . reframe the negatives into positives . . . engage people to make things happen . . . balance the long term and the short term. Can you sum up all that in a word or two?"

He thought for a moment. "Responsibility," he said at last.

"Exactly," Frances affirmed. "And the opposite of responsibility is blame. If *Think Inc!* is assuming responsibility for one's thoughts, feelings, beliefs, time, and performance, then Stink Inc. is blaming and whining about everyone and everything. People with Stink Inc. are foul and to be avoided."

They laughed. The man reiterated, "Responsibility

versus blame. Absolutely. People able and willing to accept responsibility are special. Tell me more."

"*Think Inc!* is the essential mindset of the On-Purpose Business. It's like the light switch. We have to want to turn it on. Responsibility requires ownership of the outcome. When the outcomes aren't favorable, it's simple to blame it on someone or some circumstance. People with *Think Inc!* know that negative outcomes aren't failures, they're only learning experiences. With blame, even the learning experience is lost."

Frances continued, "Some people believe *Think Inc!* doesn't apply to them. Discounting the business side of things is a big mistake! Every job is really a business.

"I'll give you an example. In my industry there are real estate agents and brokers. Many people see themselves as just that, an agent or broker. A *Think Inc!* person would see herself as a business owner who works in the real estate industry. Seeing oneself as a business rather than an agent is a subtle yet vital distinction."

The man nodded his understanding, and Frances continued, "In this way the insurance agent doesn't run an agency, he runs a business. The receptionist runs a PR business, not a switchboard. The delivery person operates a delivery business. With *Think Inc!* everyone runs a business: nurses, pastors, teachers, salespeople, assembly line people—it makes no difference. It takes a mindset of seeing yourself as a business. Every job is a business when you have a *Think Inc!* mindset.

"But most people don't."

"Why is that?" he asked.

"Owners have to think differently. They run the whole show, so they're forced to be strategic thinkers. For most people, strategic thinking is the furthest thing from their minds. They focus on tasks within their job. *Think Inc!* people focus on adding value, doing what's best, selling, building the team, and being On-Purpose."

The man agreed. "You're right. An employee mindset is nearsighted and accepts what comes along. A person with a *Think Inc!* mindset creates situations. Presidents need to be strategic thinkers. In most businesses only a handful of people think strategically. Everyone else falls in line."

Frances agreed. "Right! Imagine how powerful it is when everyone learns and uses the Four Pillars as the president of his or her own business—from entry level new hires to top management. Imagine a company filled with *Think Inc!* people."

"That would be awesome," the man replied. "But I have a question. How do you get managers, let alone front-line people, to think like business owners?"

"That," said a wide-grinning Frances, "is what Pillar Three, the Method, will provide you. Remember, *Think Inc!* is only one of the Four Pillars. Individually, each is potent; yet in combination they're totally on-purpose."

"I understand," the man said. "Bob told me that *Think Inc!* changed your life. How so?"

"The R. D. Scott Company regularly spins off businesses by team members and supports them in various ways. That's how my business got started. I was using *Think Inc!* and saw an opportunity outside the company to start a business."

"They just let you go?" asked the man.

Frances explained, "When I came to work here nine years ago in the personnel area, it was a small, fast-growing business. We were hiring and relocating lots of people here. This is my hometown; I know e-v-e-r-y-b-o-d-y. I'm like an ambassador.

"I loved relocating people here, and I saw an opportunity to start a relocation business. Bob and I talked about it, and he staked my business with his relocations and a *Think Inc!* mindset. My initiative paid off. Within days of securing my real estate license I had my first contract; I also had more fun and made more money than I did the entire month before. The rest is history."

The man sat on the edge of his seat in wonder. "In my company, you would have been fired for proposing that."

Frances smiled. "That's crazy. If initiative is the stuff of presidents, then conformity is the stuff of Stink Inc. Bob and I both won. Bob needed a great relocation service to grow his company because a failed relocation cripples the business and disrupts a family and career. By encouraging and supporting my business, we both excelled. Each of us does more of what we do best more profitably. Pretty logical, right?"

"No doubt," the man agreed.

"Bob placed two conditions on my departure. First, create the best relocation business possible. Done!

"Second, share the opportunity. I came to discover this was more than an altruistic gesture. It makes for great business. I've helped launch a home builder, a property insurance agent, a home remodeler, a landscaper, a painter . . . the list goes on and on. Do you think I get referrals! You bet!"

The man jumped in. "A sales force you don't pay — kind of like your on-purpose "pin" pals, right?"

Frances laughed her agreement.

A knock on the conference room door was followed by Bob Scott emerging from behind it. "Have you mastered *Think Inc!*?" he cheerfully asked the man.

"Yes, Bob. Frances is great. *Think Inc!* is really about

opening the minds and lives of people to new possibilities. As one of the Four Pillars of the On-Purpose Business, this deep-seated sense of responsibility really hit home with me."

"I'd say you learned your lessons. Say goodby to Frances, your On-Purpose Partner, and let's go see Hal Trudy."

The man thanked Frances. Their time together had been short, but her influence would last a lifetime.

## THE PARK BENCH

Bob ushered the man into his office and outside through a set of double doors. Across the street from the R. D. Scott Company was a large public park with wonderful old trees and blooming flowers. Bob confided, "This park is my retreat from the world. I walk here to exercise and clear my thoughts."

Stepping into the fresh air felt pleasant. The aroma of fresh-cut grass filled the air. A gardener pushed an ancient rotary-blade lawn mower on a small grassy knoll in the distance. The man delighted in the metal-upon-metal sharpening sound of the rotary blades snipping the grass. It reminded him of growing up in simpler days. The gardener gave a friendly wave to Bob as they crossed the street. Bob returned the greeting.

The man appreciated Bob's investment of his time, expertise, and relationships. Meeting these noble men and women offered hope that acts of service would remain the true gold standard. They approached a bench under the limbs of an ancient live oak tree. It was surrounded by bouquets of impatiens growing from terra cotta pots. The man couldn't help but comment, "This is beautiful, and so peaceful."

"It's a special place. Have a seat," Bob said, offering the park bench. "Hal will be along to see you. I have a plane to catch. Hal will take care of you. We'll talk again soon, after you've had time to absorb all you're learning."

With that they shook hands. Bob left for the airport. The man sat waiting for Hal.

# 10

# PILLAR THREE — THE SERVICE MODEL

▼

*Rosebud!*

**The last word spoken by Citizen Kane**
*from the movie Citizen Kane*

Admiring his surroundings, the man relaxed on the bench as he awaited the arrival of Hal Trudy. His peaceful interlude waned as a disturbing stream of thoughts crept in. *Things are bad at the business. Sales are dropping, morale is low, and production problems persist. The GEOMay contract is all but lost. We've got to act fast.*

The man stood and paced to a nearby rose garden in hopes of quieting his mind. Sniffing from rose to rose momentarily quenched the fire raging in his thoughts.

"Ah-h, you like my roses," came a kind voice from behind the man. He turned to see the gardener's proud smile.

"Is this your handiwork?" asked the man.

"I accept partial responsibility," said the gardener, pointing toward heaven. "I get lots of help from the Upstairs Boss. Roses of many varieties are my passion." The gardener was in his seventies. His youthful stride and movements appeared to be those of a younger man. Up close, though, his age showed on a sun-worn face set with sparkling eyes and a flashing smile. His trim, fit body was covered by a khaki city parks uniform.

The man praised, "These roses are beautiful!"

"Thank you. In caring for roses, I also care for myself."

The man said, "This is a haven in the midst of a crazy world. What a gift you give, sir. I envy you because your work makes a difference in the world."

The gardener furrowed his brow. "And your work is not so meaningful?"

The man swung his head in a resigned manner. "No need to burden you with my problems. I'm meeting a man here shortly who I'm trusting will show me a better method."

"Sir, it's no burden. Helping cultivate the roses within

you keeps me on-purpose." Grinning, the gardener extended his right hand. "Hi! My name is Hal Trudy."

The man was embarrassed. Introducing himself, he apologized for his presumptuous behavior.

Hal answered, "Don't apologize; learn a lesson."

"Don't judge a book by its cover," the man suggested.

"Perhaps." Hal smiled. "The bigger lesson is to see your work as an extension of your purpose. Regardless of the humbleness of the duty performed, you can be on-purpose.

"First, you must value your work regardless of the pay scale the world places on it. It is inherently profitable when it is on-purpose. Two thousand years ago a wise man posed the question, 'For what does it matter, if you gain the world, but lose your soul?'"

The man asked Hal, "What if my work causes me to lose my soul?"

"Only you can choose to lose your soul. Meaning is not found in power, pleasures, position, or prestige. Purpose is first a matter of the heart. Move toward your purpose, and TOP Opportunities steadfastly emerge. Life and time are so perishable."

Hal held the stem of a rosebud and snipped it from the bush. Handing it to the man, he continued, "We're like a fresh-cut rose. So little time until we wilt away."

"Thank you for the advice," the man said. "Does your purpose statement involve roses by chance?"

"Yes!" replied Hal. "My purpose statement is 'Cultivating Roses.' You see, roses require cultivation and care to bloom. Roses are the flowers in this park and also people waiting to bloom brilliantly. Both need proper care, nourishment, pruning, and attention. We all have a higher potential; I cultivate it in roses and people. Roses are my elegantly meaningful metaphor for humanity and me."

"I see. You cultivate roses everywhere, don't you?" supposed the man.

"Yes, that's true. Some conditions are more favorable than others for living one's purpose." Smiling now, Hal offered, "As in my little garden here, to improve conditions sometimes one deals with the fertile manure of experiences that smudge yet enrich our character."

Both men laughed. The man was struck by this gardener's strength, humor, and earthy wisdom. He invited Hal to sit under the magnificent oak. Then he said, "Please teach me about Pillar Three—the Method of the On-Purpose Business."

Hal picked up a long, thin stick and playfully maneuvered it from hand to hand while speaking. "The Method is the Service Model. This on-purpose prototype provides a systematic means to develop a purpose statement into an operational reality, that is, to be on-purpose." With that, Hal pointed the long stick toward the man's chest as an old schoolmaster might do to a student and asked, "Ready to get started?"

"Yes, sir," snapped the man smartly.


## THE SERVICE MODEL

"The Service Model is common sense." Hal half cupped his mouth with his hand, leaned toward the man, and whispered, "Unfortunately, common sense isn't so common these days." They both smiled.

Hal resumed his teaching. "How do you think the model got its name?"

"The Service Model?" asked the man. "Is this a trick question?"

"No, I assume nothing."

"The Service Model is about service," answered the man.

"Right," Hal confirmed. "Do you appreciate the importance of this relative to creating an On-Purpose Business?"

"I hadn't thought of the connection," the man replied.

"Purpose is a service concept. Recall that the generic start of a purpose statement is 'I exist to serve by . . . ,' or, for an organization, 'We exist to serve by. . . .' This is a different perspective than some who believe a business exists only to make money. Here the premium is on service, and profit is a necessary by-product."

The man's eyes opened wide. "This is very different."

Hal agreed, "Yes, radically different. Service is purpose in action. Even businesses that are customer service–minded may miss the mark. They typically talk in terms of customer service. Actually there are three tests of service. First, does it serve a higher good or power? Second, does it serve the person providing the service? Third, does it serve another person? In businesses we call them customers. All three must be served for it to be on-purpose."

"That's a high standard," the man said.

"Yep!" said Hal, summarily dismissing any further discussion on the point. He brought the question full circle. "So why is it called the Service Model?"

The man repeated, "Purpose is a service concept."

"Good, but not good enough. Hint, hint," prodded Hal. "What's a model?"

The man said, "A model is a set of plans, a design, a pattern or prototype for others to follow. It's a scaled miniature of something larger, like a model airplane. It's an ideal version, like a model citizen."

"Yes," Hal agreed. "In fact, the Service Model is all those definitions. Now put it together, service and model."

"I get it," the man said. "The Service Model is a plan or

design for putting purpose into action. It is also a pattern for others to follow so they can duplicate it. It is also a miniature of something larger. It's an ideal to strive toward."

"Terrific," Hal commended. "The Service Model is a strategic, operational, and tactical tool enabling predictable service."

Hal stood up from the park bench and stretched his hands high in the air. "Let's take a stroll. I need to turn some sprinklers off in another part of the park." They walked.

"One more thing: Like learning anything new, it will take time, practice, and coaching to master the Service Model. As you master it, you'll more consistently render model service." Hal gave an impish grin and winked. "A little play on words."

# 11

# THE SERVICE LEVELS

▼

*Some people walk in the rain.*
*Others just get wet.*

**Roger Miller**
*Singer and Songwriter*

As the two men strolled the park grounds, the man reflected on his lessons. The Four Pillars were simple and sensible. The Service Model, however, was still just a concept. Having no mental image of it, he struggled to relate. He broached the topic with Hal.

"May I see the Service Model?"

Hal turned and smiled at him. "I thought you'd never ask. Give me a minute to get these sprinklers." As Hal worked, he told the man, "The Four Pillars of the On-Purpose Business made me a wealthy man. It can do the same for you. Just remember the difference between being rich and being wealthy. Riches are in the pockets, and wealth is in the heart. I'm blessed with both."

Hal placed his arm affectionately around the man's shoulder. "Many people don't understand business. Business is a high and noble calling in which you risk much to give much. Finance, marketing, operations, and all that—they're pieces of the model.

"After today, you'll have insight. You're still a way from mastering the model, but at least you'll be aware. I call it insightful ignorance—you'll know what you don't know."

The man felt some relief and encouragement. "So, show me the Service Model already."

"The Five P's—they're the progressive steps to building the Service Model. With these you'll analyze, build, and correct the business. Here are the Five P's in order: Purpose, Plan, People, Processes, and Performance, all to serve the Customer."

Hal knelt to the ground and began using the long stick as a writing tool. The man fell to one knee. They looked like two sandlot football players designing plays in the dirt. Hal wrote a large *V*.

"This is the Service Model. This large *V* represents

'values.' At the base of the *V* let's write 'Purpose,' representing the purpose of the organization. Next, we'll fill in the other P's."

## THE SERVICE MODEL™

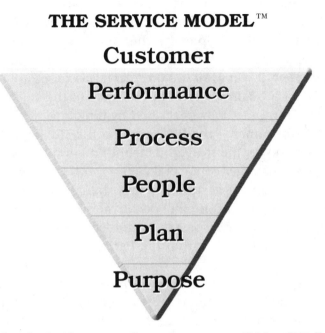

Customer
Performance
Process
People
Plan
Purpose

Hal finished. The man admired it, saying, "I like it! Tell me more."

"Purpose — this is the Purpose Principle. State the purpose of the organization as 'P(o).' It's the nucleus. The Purpose Principle links to the Service Model. Without this linkage, the entire Service Model is empty.

"Plan — an on-purpose plan includes positioning, visions, values, and missions emanating from the purpose. Your position is the place you occupy in the mind of your customer. It's very important. Remember to include other strategic, operational, and tactical plans. There may be several key outcomes or goals to list as well.

"People—you need a team to engage with the purpose and plan. Ideally, these are TOP Performers, especially in the beginning.

"Processes—when average people are asked what makes up a business, they mention the functional areas within the firm. Typically, this includes accounting, finance, marketing, human resources, and operations, to name a few. If you want to know what processes are most valued in a business, look at the titles of the vice presidents. They're usually described by function.

"Performance—the line between the Customer and Performance is the proverbial front line of the business. All direct customer contact takes place at the performance level of the Service Model. The prior four P's merely position the organization for performance. Salespeople, receptionists, delivery people, customer-service personnel, and others all work within the Performance area of the business. The intent is for them to succeed by design.

"Customer—for us to be on-purpose, we serve customers, clients, patients, guests, or whatever noun is appropriate to the organization. Serving customers is the lifeblood of a business and the ultimate expression of its purpose. Customers are the outward and visible recipients of an inner-rewarding service rendered; that's called being on-purpose.

"There you have the Five P's of the Service Model. It is the motherboard, to borrow a computer term, upon which all organizations create, build, and dream. Each service level grows naturally from the next. It's as natural as seeds producing flowers. The Service Model borrows from nature's growth process."

The man responded, "If I understand it correctly, every performance-related issue in a business actually has roots in the purpose of the organization."

"Exactly," Hal commended. "A business is like a rose-bush. In other words, roses don't bloom unless the roots, bush, and stems are healthy. The entire system requires cultivation to produce the buds.

"In contrast, consider a business that starts wanting 'flowers' but won't feed the plant or prepare the soil. That's a business focused on the Performance level only. Shallow roots can actually work . . . for a while! But these are false results. The plant can't endure hardships, and the harvest will be scarce.

"Armed with the Service Model, how might you start a business?"

"I would . . . wow!" the man interrupted himself. "This is a unique vantage point. I would define the purpose of the organization by completing the phrase 'I exist to serve by. . . .' This would be tested with the customer, the community, the business, and me. Then I would create a plan with dreams and vision for the company and a positioning with our customers."

Hal nodded approvingly.

"Next, I would gather a team to help make the plan a reality and put the processes in place to perform for the customers."

"Excellent!" Hal approved. "One more question for you to ponder. How does strategy fit with being an On-Purpose Business?"

A stream of thoughts erupted from the man, "The Service Model . . . Purpose is a service concept . . . the Five P's. . . ."

Suddenly, the man's face lit up. "I've got it. Alignment! The entire organization is aligned with the purpose of the organization; that's an On-Purpose Business. Then, the

Five P's are aligned to serve the customer. As a result, the business is on-purpose, rather than off-purpose. I guess you might even say the customers are on-purpose."

"Yes, you nailed it!" congratulated Hal.

The man added, "It's an amazingly different approach; yet it's just common sense once you see it. It even feels healthier and more wholesome. Maybe the design and order are what make it all seem so manageable." In all my years in business, I've never seen the big picture so clearly, or simply.

Hal's eyes twinkled with a mentor's delight. The man, in fact, understood a great deal of the Service Model. Hal knew the next lesson would stretch him even further.

### "V" IS FOR VALUE

"In the beginning, you may recall, I said the Service Model is in the shape of a *V* for value. Any organization must add value to survive, and I know your company is facing survival issues right now.

"Earlier, you touched on a vital point: TOP Customers. I want you to meet a dynamo of a woman. Her name is Pam Dimes. She's a value-adding natural. Listen to her. You need what she has to share to turn around the company. Call her." He handed the man a scrap of paper with Pam's name and number. "She's a business owner. Let's talk again, after you meet Pam. Deliberate on what you've learned and how to put this into practice in your company."

"Thanks, Hal. I will. I learned so much today. I don't think I'll ever look at the business the same way."

They shook hands. Hal headed toward the rose garden. The man returned to work. He called Pam and arranged an appointment for the following week.

Back in his office the man sat at his desk writing in

the pages of his journal. He contemplated the Purpose Principle, *Think Inc!*, and the Service Model. Order was emerging from chaos.

What were the future implications of this new approach? How would he put all he had learned into practice? He wanted everyone in the company to use the Four Pillars. Becoming an On-Purpose Business would be a major shift in the corporate culture and method of operation.

A knock on his open door broke his thoughts. Jackie popped her head into his office and said, "Mrs. Taylor is on the phone."

Raising the phone to his ear, he greeted his former boss's wife. "Hi, Mrs. Taylor. How's Fred?"

In a soft voice she answered, "It's his heart again. I'm at the hospital. I wanted you to know since you were kind enough to visit last time. No need to visit this time."

"Is he all right?" the man asked politely.

Mrs. Taylor's voice broke. "It's serious. Please let everyone in the company know. To Fred, they're his family."

She continued, "Our children are helping. I'm staying by Fred until he awakens. He'll want to talk. Despite his failing health, these have been happy days for us. In the short time since his retirement he's become a free man without the chains of the company weighing on him."

They exchanged goodbys. He hung up the phone. A strange set of emotions whirled inside him. Fred worked all his life only to have his heart fail a few weeks after retiring. And Fred's "chains" were now his! This wasn't the way the man wanted it to be for him.

Jackie walked into his office. "Is Fred okay?" she asked.

"No. He's back in the hospital." He asked Jackie to spread the word about Fred.

# 12

# CUSTOMER CONFLUENCE

▼

*Wisdom is the art of living
skillfully in whatever actual
conditions we find ourselves.*

**Eugene H. Peterson**
*The Message: Proverbs*

J ackie announced to the man, "Pam Dimes is here to see you."

"Thanks!" The man headed to the lobby to greet Pam. The week since his meeting with Hal Trudy had flown by quickly. Fred was home recovering but still weak.

As he walked, the man considered that his company was in bad shape and getting worse. Tension was high. Earlier in the week an executive team meeting had ended with an argument between Sam Cellars, the vice president of sales and marketing, and Pat Squires, the vice president of operations. He thought, *Perhaps Pam has answers to help me focus the team on matters at hand.*

Spotting Pam in the lobby was easy. She was a striking sight in her bright red tailored business suit. Set against her white pleated blouse and bow was an elegant gold chain. They introduced themselves. While showing her to his office, the man inquired, "Please tell me about your business."

Pam began, "I'm an independent distributor with a direct sales company. I've built a large sales team over the years."

Arriving at his office, he introduced Pam and Jackie. "Please hold my calls," he said to Jackie, then after entering his office and closing the door, he and Pam sat down across from each other at a small round table in the corner. He asked, "Why does Hal call you a 'value-adding natural'?"

"Because I've got it figured out," Pam confidently offered.

"How so?" asked the man.

"Which of your customers are the most on-purpose for your business?" she quizzed.

"I haven't got a clue," the man answered. "A lot of factors come into play."

Pam stopped him with her hand. "Excuses! You've got to know which customers are the most on-purpose for you. They're the ones receiving the highest value for your product or service. An on-purpose businessperson must be able to pinpoint his or her best customers with high accuracy."

"How?" the man asked.

"Look at your Service Model. It was designed to serve a specific set of customers."

"We don't really have one," the man answered. "We treat all customers alike."

"You have a Service Model by default," Pam retorted. "Customers value your products and services differently. While you may not distinguish between one customer and another, they do distinguish your business from others."

"I see," said the man. "So our Service Model gears us to be more suited to some customers than others."

"Exactly," Pam affirmed.

"So how do I get more of 'our' type of customers?" asked the man.

Pam beamed. "Excellent question. The phenomenon of 'our type of customers' is called Customer Confluence. It happens when need and solution intersect."

The man joked, "The On-Purpose Prospect meets the On-Purpose Provider."

"Precisely," Pam indicated. "That's good!"

"Thanks. But how?" the man asked again.

Pam explained, "Every level in the Service Model is a prelude to Performance for the Customer. Our Purpose, Plan, People, and Processes have all been geared to serve a specific customer segment. When that customer appears, no one, I repeat, no one is able to offer comparable value. The value of our performance depends upon our preparation. The Service Model is our preparation to serve the customer.

"Think about when you've shopped for a service or product. Have you ever found a doctor whose expertise and manner matched your needs? Or maybe your wife found that perfect dress for a special occasion. Or was it finding the right school for a special-needs child? Consider what it was like when you finally found what you were looking for."

The man answered, "Joy, relief, good fortune, peace. . . ." Pam encouraged him with quick hand motioning to keep expressing himself. "My needs were understood, even anticipated and met."

"That," said Pam with authority, "is Customer Confluence. And when more of your customers experience the feelings you've just described, then you'll be well on your way to being an On-Purpose Business."

The man supposed, "And without Customer Confluence . . . all that's left as a basis of determining the value is price. Right?"

"Exactly. And price is a small, yet important, aspect of any transaction. So again I pose the question: Who are your TOP Customers?"

"I need to get with my people. I can't answer that question."

Pam encouraged him. "Once you can articulate who they are, what they want, and what they do, then you'll serve them like no other. Eventually they will become your best referral source for more customers like themselves because you provide the best value-added service or product."

The man observed, "I realize now that our company has a certain set of customers with whom we consistently excel. To fully leverage our investment in the Service Model, we need more of 'our kind of customers.'"

"Yes!" Pam enthused. "It makes no sense to keep on reinventing the business to satisfy a revolving door of onetime customers. Now you can fully utilize your Technical and Tingle alignment to the fullest potential. Customer Confluence results in repeat business and referrals because high value is embedded throughout the Service Model, all the way from the Purpose to the front line with the Customer. This is the business equivalent of a divine appointment." Interlocking her fingers from both hands, she dramatically announced, "Finally, we've found one another!"

The man sat back in his chair. "Wow! I've never heard it expressed like that. You're right, it is a magical moment. It's almost romantic."


## THE FRONT LINE

Pam continued, "Many people talk about the front line of the business. We're going to define it as the line on the Service Model between the Customer and the Performance levels. Front line employees work in direct contact with customers.

"Everything in the Service Model is a prelude to Performance along the front line. Customer value is either gained or lost along the front line. Ideally, the customer's interaction with the front line is seamlessly smooth because of Customer Confluence. When that happens, it's like you're manufacturing customers."

"Manufacturing customers?" he queried.

"Not manufacturing like you're thinking of it. Remember, we're talking about adding value. Manufacturing, as I'm using it, means creating predictable, desired outcomes from a certain set of inputs and processes."

"Okay, that makes sense," he agreed.

"Good." She smiled. "The On-Purpose Business is like a precise Swiss watch. Hidden behind the face of the watch are movements, gears, and jewels hard at work. Watches must be predictably accurate. An On-Purpose Business via the Service Model provides similar reliability."

"Impressive, but is it realistic?" he questioned.

"Realistically, we're enhancing predictability, not creating certainty. Machines and watches can be crafted to tight tolerances. People, well," she said, smirking, "they're not so tolerable."

"Point well taken," conceded the man with a laugh.

Pam continued, "Customer Confluence is all about enabling each party in the relationship and transaction simply to do more of what they do best more profitably."

"Pillar Four!" The man recognized the phrase.

"Yes, Pillar Four," Pam confirmed.

The man pressed, "Go back for a second. You mentioned relationship and transaction. How do they relate to Customer Confluence?"

Pam explained, "Good question. The exchange of value is created in two ways: the transaction and the relationship. Ideally, value is high from both."

"What do you mean by transaction?" questioned the man.

"The transaction is the deal. It's the act of doing business — the contract, sale, or engagement for a product or service in exchange for consideration, monetary or otherwise. Typically, this is easily identified."

"And," asked the man, "how does relationship influence value?"

"Relationship is the feeling before, during, and long after the transaction is complete. It is more difficult to gauge directly."

"So," concluded the man, "if there's high Customer Confluence, then there's value added by both the transaction and the relationship. Right?"

"Right," Pam affirmed. "In plain English, it's a good deal for everybody."

She proceeded, "Would you prefer to call on a customer cold or with a referral?"

"A referral, any day," he answered.

"Why?"

"It's a definite advantage because trust is more readily established."

"And is trust valuable?" Pam asked.

"Absolutely," the man agreed and laughed. "You're good. I see how relationships add value to the transaction."

Pam acknowledged the compliment. "Thank you."

The man admitted, "Our front line team members are at a disadvantage because they don't have the benefit of a clearly defined Service Model supporting their efforts. In essence, we've sabotaged their best efforts because the root of our challenge lies deeper in the Service Model. Now I know where to enhance our Performance. These *are* potent insights."

Pam beamed with pride. "You're welcome," she said. "I figured a person in your position knew everything about business. I'm flattered I could help."

He rolled his eyes and said, "You'd be surprised what I've been learning. Hal was right. You are a value-adding natural. Customer Confluence sums it all up neatly.

"Thanks again for coming." The man walked Pam to the lobby and said goodby.

▼ ▼ ▼

## THE APPOINTED TIME

As the man returned from the lobby, Jackie reminded him, "You're late for your 'appointment.'"

Looking at his watch, he gasped. "I lost track of the time!" he said. "Call Jay, Tom, and Betty at Birdwood. Let them know I'm on my way. We're having lunch first, then playing eighteen. I'm gone."

Jackie laughed. "I know the routine," she said. "I'll take care of everything. Go!"

He ran to his car. This regular monthly golf foursome was made up of his company's banker, CPA, and insurance agent. Shortly after being tapped as company president, he had brought together these key advisers to integrate their relationships of trust. So far it was working.

Wheeling his car from the parking lot, he fixed his mind on Customer Confluence. It was an eye-opening concept.

At the country club, a woman in a white minivan loaded with kids pulled out of a parking space right by the door to the men's locker room. He grabbed the space, dashed in, and changed into his golf clothes. Quickly he joined the others at the grill for lunch. Ever-thoughtful Jackie had gone the extra mile and ordered him a chef salad. He and the salad arrived at the same time. He was back on schedule.

They finished lunch and moved to the first tee. It was a sunny, perfect day for golf. The foursome had a great time. The man was thrilled with the way he played. For a hacker, he scored a rare birdie on number five and had six pars. Never mind the ten on number eight and the triple bogeys on numbers twelve and sixteen. He was having a rare, carefree afternoon away from the office. What a relaxing joy!

Walking off number eighteen, the golf pro emerged from the pro shop. "Your assistant, Jackie, called. She asked that you call her as soon as possible. It's important. She left her home phone number."

"Thanks," he said as he took the message slip. He told the others, "Let me make a quick phone call. I'll see you in the clubhouse."

Once in the men's locker room, he dialed Jackie's number. It rang twice and then he heard "Hello." Jackie's voice lacked her usual perky punch.

He said, "Hi! It's me. What's up?"

"Bad news, Fred Taylor died this afternoon," Jackie said. "Fred's son called the office to let you know. There was nothing you could do, so I figured you might as well enjoy your golf game. I hope you don't mind?"

"You did the right thing, Jackie." He hung up the phone and crashed onto a bench by the lockers. With his head in his hands he began crying. Despite all of Fred's shortcomings, he was the Old Man, the patriarch of the company, and a legend in the community. Their relationship spanned more than fifteen years.

His heart ached. He had never anticipated this emotional response. Things were different; he was changing. The legendary Frederick W. Taylor was dead.

He gathered his thoughts and called Jackie back. "Thanks for tracking me down. Do you know the details of the funeral?"

# 13

# THE MODEL WAY

▼

*When one door of happiness
closes, another opens; but often
we look so long at the closed door
that we do not see the one which
has been opened.*

**Helen Keller (1880–1969)**
*Deaf and Blind Activist*

A week had passed since Fred's death. The man spied Hal Trudy raking leaves near an azalea cluster down a path leading to a canopy of oaks, magnolias, and pines. "Hello!" he shouted to Hal.

Looking up from his work, Hal recognized him. They greeted and shook hands.

"Sorry to hear about Fred Taylor," Hal sympathized.

"Thanks. He was buried three days ago. The funeral was surprisingly uplifting. The pastor called it a resurrection service. The church was decked out in white. Even Mrs. Taylor wore a white dress!

"We sang some inspiring songs. I remembered 'Onward, Christian Soldiers' from my childhood. Another one was 'I Sing a Song of the Saints of God.' It has a catchy hook." He crooned the words.

Hal picked up the line and offered an off-key rendition: ". . . and one was a soldier, and one was a priest, and one was slain by a fierce, wild beast. And all of them were saints of God, and I hope to be one, too."

"You know it!" the man declared with amazement.

"Good stuff," Hal proclaimed, then added, "music is not my gift, though. Ain't nothing in 'cultivating roses' about singing."

After a chuckle, the man mused, "Fred's funeral was different. I expected . . . well, you know, a funeral . . . dark, somber, and sad. The sense of hope and renewal was a sharp contrast from the life of the Fred Taylor I knew." They chatted a bit longer about it.

Now leaning on his rake, Hal commented, "Fascinating. Maybe Fred finally began living in the midst of his dying. That's the Easter message, isn't it? There's always hope, no matter how bleak the situation appears."

In a moment Hal lamented, "If only more people would

choose the path of hope and choose it sooner. Perhaps you'll learn from this?"

The man didn't understand. Yet he knew Hal meant him well. From this reflective mood, he redirected the conversation. "Pam Dimes really helped me. She used Customer Confluence to make the Service Model real. At my business we've spent so much time fixing symptoms that I never realized the true source of our problems lay deeper. All of our symptom fixing created a variety of side effects, which needed a set of policies and procedures that drew us even further off-purpose.

"We're unfocused. What a mess! Now I have a schematic to build from the foundation of the business to the customer."

"Great," Hal said with a smile. "What else did you learn?"

"Customer Confluence intrigued me. With our limited resources we can't afford to build a Service Model for every conceivable customer. So I'm focusing our efforts on the On-Purpose Customers. We'll build our Service Model to serve them. It's bound to be more rewarding.

"I'm beginning with the GEOMay Company. We've fouled up that relationship."

"You're learning your lessons well," Hal commented.

The man thought, *Hal's so happy and positive. What a great guy. I can't imagine what my career would have been like if I had worked for a person like him.*

## PODS OF PURPOSE

By then Hal was into a new thought. "There's another dimension to the Service Model," he said. "I'm going to ask you a question, and promise me you'll think for thirty seconds before you answer."

The man nodded his agreement.

"How many seeds are in an apple?"

The man started to answer, but Hal motioned for him to wait. The time passed, and then Hal called for the answer.

The man guessed, "About ten."

Hal shook his head. "You're in a cash mindset rather than an equity mindset. *Think Inc!* Try again; think big this time."

The man thought for a few moments. Finally, he said, "Hal, hand me the stick so I can hit myself." Hal chuckled. "An apple holds unlimited seeds. One seed in an apple could become another apple tree, which in turn produces more apples with seeds, which in turn produce more trees, more apples, more seeds, and the cycle goes on and on forever."

"Yes!" said Hal as he victoriously thrust his right fist in the air. "You're making progress. Building an organization is the same way. The Service Model is like a seed. So how many 'seeds' are in a business?"

"Unlimited," answered the man.

"Yes, and purpose is the germ of the seed. Most people have a pretty good idea of how plants grow; yet few people understand how an organization grows." Hal's speech quieted to a near whisper. "The fact is that most people entrusted with leading an organization just haven't been through the cultivation process enough times to recognize their way. That's the value of experience, mistakes, observation, and time."

The man moved nearer to Hal and said, "So, like a seed, the Service Model potentially holds an unlimited number of other Service Models. It's a metaphor for the organizational development process?"

"Yes," Hal confirmed. "The business has a Service Model, as can every person in the business. The only difference is scope of responsibility. The CEO has broader responsibilities than a sales representative; yet each person has his or her own Service Model within the organizational Service Model."

"So the Service Model provides a structural standard?" posed the man.

"Absolutely," Hal assured. "The Service Model is a leader's road map. It can't replace experience, nor should it. It compresses learning because the responsible person now has perspective, a map, and directions. The more one travels a route, the greater the familiarity with the way.

"Most people don't have a map. Others they meet along the way are just as lost, so they're little help. Well-intentioned, yes; helpful, no. That's why I'm adamant that everyone, from the receptionist to the chairman of the board, use the Service Model to understand his or her job, the company, and the relationship of the two. People need experience using it. They need connection, belonging, and meaningful contribution. They need to know that their life and work matter. And this map is the best tool for either individual or collaborative efforts."

The man was awed. He said, "Hal, you're absolutely right! Here I am the president of this company, and so much of this is virgin territory for me. I can tell you where I've been, but mapping where I'm going . . . that's challenging. My entire career I've bounced along without a map. It's been business and career mostly by trial and error. Fortunately, I progressed because I played it conservatively. Mostly, I stumbled and felt my way along trying not to offend but never being bold."

"How sad never to be bold," Hal said with a sigh.

"On rare occasions someone special charted a short course for me. These are mentors: Mrs. Ift, my third-grade teacher; Mr. Stifler, my eighth-grade math teacher; and Mr. Davies, who just encouraged me. The professor has made a huge difference in my life. Of course my parents were the best. All of these people saw my promise and potential before I did because they had perspectives and experiences I didn't have. They elevated my sights.

"Hal, someone like Fred Taylor—shouldn't he have figured this out?"

"Fred Taylor didn't figure it out," Hal replied. "Stop blaming him, Mr. Stink Inc. He was what he was in his day. Frederick W. Taylor is dead, and so are his ways. Must we bury him again? Learn from the past, then move on. I'm sorry to have to be so blunt."

"Thank you," the man said. "I needed to hear that."

Hal stated, "Forty-eight seasons in the business taught him plenty. The problem was, only Fred knew what he knew. He was a master of the Technical and a neophyte of the Tingle. His forty-eight years on the job enabled him to declare solutions to problems, to be the answer man. Because his solutions were limited to his experiences, he confined the business to stagnation.

"His focus was isolated to the Processes and Performance levels. His idea of planning was setting sales goals and doing budgets, right?"

"Yes. You're absolutely right," the man marveled.

"Goals and budgets are Performance-level activities, outcomes of what was set up by other P's of the Service Model. Fred managed by objectives but never got to the object of the objectives—the purpose of the business. Fred wasn't alone in this manner of business. In fact, he personifies the Industrial Age mindset and method.

"To Fred, the business was the customer, sales, and systems. His blind spots were the people, plan, and purpose of the business. He was a 'get it done' driver with presidential responsibility, not really a president. He had no idea what he didn't know. For Fred, business life was a series of daily crises with only one predictable outcome," Hal reported.

"What's that?" asked the man.

"A heart attack."

"Ouch! Sad but true," agreed the man.

Hal nodded and asked, "What if Fred had known what you now know, and had acted on it?"

"Unbelievable," said the man, shaking his head. "Unbelievable where we might be today."

Hal added, "The Service Model enables more meaningful teachable moments, which grow both the person and the business. You can see on 'the map' where you fit and what your strengths and weaknesses are. A prior sense of inadequacy gives way to competence and confidence. It enables real decisions in real situations and constant learning at every level of responsibility."

"You're right!" the man exclaimed.

Hal knew the On-Purpose Business was taking root. "The Service Model is powerful," he continued. "It's like having a mental filing cabinet where you place and retrieve information and insight at will. You now possess a permanent mental plan of organizing and organization."

"Yes," the man answered, "I have that."


## THE NESTING DOLLS

The man continued. "The Service Model reminds me of those Russian nesting dolls. Pop the doll open and inside is a slightly smaller, similar doll. And inside that doll is a still smaller doll, and so on and so on."

"Yes," Hal laughed. "I love the image. The Service Model has nesting. The corporation has a Service Model. Open up the corporate model, and inside there's a nesting division model. Inside the division model is a company model, inside the company model is a department model, and inside the department model is a hard-working person with a position model. All are ideally and ultimately linked to a common purpose and set of values."

"It's awesome," the man replied. He grabbed a stick from the ground and waved it triumphantly in the air.

Hal remarked, "Cool it with the stick, though. You're making me nervous."

"Sorry, it's just that this is an interesting way to see the business as totally duplicatable. Everyone has a Service Model."


## THE SINGLE BUILDING BLOCK

The man was curious about something. "Are there other ways to use the Service Model?"

"The model has a variety of applications. Use it for strategic planning, project management, and task forces. Use it to diagnose problems and prescribe solutions. Use it to write job descriptions and position contracts. Launch a new product or service using it. Have a salesperson or receptionist design his or her job using it. The applications of the Service Model are unlimited."

"Hal," the man posed, "then big organizations are nothing more than smaller organizations, which are nothing more than clusters of individuals. The whole rests solely on a single building block — one person performing a service. The Service Model gives the power of the whole to the one, and the power of one to the whole."

"Yes," Hal agreed. "That's the power of purpose. It is why leaders like Bob Scott and I want team members to be On-Purpose Businesspersons. Personal experience with the Service Model helps us more readily relate to the issues of the corporate Service Model. As the power in a single atom is vast, so it is with the potential of one person. Combine the design qualities of the Service Model and the other Pillars — now you're talking nuclear power.

"It makes you appreciate those people in the business who see the big picture and can focus on their job responsibilities."

"Too few are capable of both," the man said.

"Wrong!" Hal corrected. "People are extremely capable. Let them see the Service Model, and they'll surprise you with just how capable they are. Your problem then is staying out of their way."

The man commented, "The Pillars are changing my entire perspective. It's like I've developed a sixth sense of understanding and insight."

"That's as it should be," Hal acknowledged. "In my years of running a business, I observed that discussions have two components: content and process. People process content differently. And each person brings different content to the process.

"The Service Model provides a common process to deal with differing content. In times of information overload, the only remaining basis for working together may be a common purpose and process."

"Hal," the man asked, "it always comes back to purpose, doesn't it?"

"Of course it does."

Hal continued, "You've learned a great deal in the past few weeks. Let's reflect for a moment. You've been exposed to a new meaning, mindset, and method to conduct your business. Your career and business will take on new vitality and insight provided you do your part. Knowledge without action is nothing.

"I appreciate the urgency in your business right now, but there's yet another person you need to see. You're already acquainted with each other. His name is Perry James. After you see Perry, it's time to act. We can get to Pillar Four later."

The man tingled with excitement. Hal was right. His working knowledge of the Four Pillars had already shed insights and wisdom on several situations. Once blind to an entire body of knowledge, he now was sighted. How many more people were like him? How many of them were working at his company? As executives?

# 14

# THE VALUE OF VALUES

▼

*If there were a controlling power outside the universe . . . the only way we could expect it to show itself would be inside ourselves as an influence or a command trying to get us to behave in a certain way.*

**C. S. Lewis**
*Mere Christianity*

Driving to his lunch meeting with Perry James, the man admired the sunny, crisp fall day. He thought, *Glad I arranged to meet him at The Sidewalk Cafe.* Perry was a retired business executive who served on the boards of several businesses and nonprofit organizations. He and the man had a deep friendship.

Parking his car at the curb next to the cafe, the man saw Perry already sitting at a table shaded by a large umbrella sipping an iced tea and reading a magazine. When he walked up and greeted him, Perry rose. "Good to see you, old friend," Perry said. "With my travels the past few months and the arrival of my first grandchild, I've missed our time together."

They chatted awhile, and the man admired Perry's pictures of his granddaughter. Then Perry said, "Congratulations, Mr. President! A well-deserved honor and great opportunity." In a soft afterword he added, "I was sad to hear of Fred Taylor's death."

"We'll all miss Fred," the man said.

The men placed their lunch orders. The man promptly proceeded to the agenda. "Hal Trudy suggested we talk about values as they relate to the Service Model. What's the role of values?"

Perry nodded. "Hal's right. Values are our internal priorities. What else have others told you?"

Recalling his conversation with the professor, the man added, "Purpose holds it all, even values. Values reside in our throat and gut. Hal explained that values are the nutrients that feed the organization."

"Good," Perry confirmed. "The Purpose Principle, this heart-to-heart alignment, transcends even values. It enables people of diverse cultures, races, social circles, or political parties to lay aside differing values to advance a common purpose. Upon this linkage rest the values, visions, missions, and outcomes of the organization."

The man observed, "Sounds good on paper. How's it really work?"

"Challenging, always challenging," Perry admitted with a smile. "Yet, try organizing people around values—or anything, for that matter—without a purpose.

"Values are the instilled right and wrong within an organization. These values may or may not be ethical. You know, 'honor among thieves.'" They both laughed.

"Purpose," Perry stressed, "is always positive, life-giving, and truthful—God's will instead of our will, if you will. Values form a thin boundary within which people are free to act."

"Boundaries? Tell me about them," asked the man.

"Boundaries let us know when we cross the border from right to wrong. Without clear boundaries, things go afield. Undefined values limit the ability of an organization to serve and grow. Inevitably, undefined values lead to situational values, which are out of context from the whole. They're no longer values, only recommendations . . . a recipe for disaster.

"Instill values, and you've improved the chances of people having right actions and spirits under pressure. One *must* do what's right rather than what's expedient."

"What's expedient versus what's right," echoed the man. "I'll remember that. So how do I apply this?"

"Write the values for your business. Violating values is just plain bad business," Perry stated matter-of-factly. "A Service Model without boundaries eventually drifts from its TOP Customers. For those customers, the departure from values signals a drop in value. Soon the customer base drifts toward off-purpose customers. Profits plummet because the economies of the Service Model are lost. All that's left with which to compete is price."

"That says it all," the man nodded in agreement.

## DETERMINING VALUES

The waiter appeared with their lunches. As they ate, Perry pulled a pen from his pocket and drew the Service Model. "The V shape of the model is a reminder that values form the boundary for creating an On-Purpose Business." With his pen he wrote next to the model the letters A-L-U-E-S, so it would spell VALUES. "Let's explore how values work in the Service Model.

"Values are determined, communicated, checked and engaged, aligned, and, finally, transferred within the Service Model. Let's go through it step by step.

"Step one is values determination. From the point of Purpose at the base of the Service Model comes the Plan. In the Plan, the leader ascertains the values, as well as the vision, missions, and outcomes.

"Step two is values communication. The values are shared and woven into the fabric of the Plan, People, and Processes. You form the business culture by integrating values into the design and flow of the organization.

"Step three is values checking and engaging. Here we compare the values of the organization with our personal values to check for alignment. The results are like a traffic signal. Red means stop and don't go any further; yellow means proceed with caution; green means go forward. When you advance, this is a decision to engage with the values of the organization.

"Step four is values alignment. This is the integration of the values of the person and the organization. Ideally they're already compatible. Reality mirrors theory when the alignment is high. The Plan, People, Process, and Performance for serving the customer are aligned. This is personal and corporate integrity.

"Step five is value transfer. This is the front line transaction and relationship-producing value. At this point the entire model has been designed to serve the Customer with the greatest possible value, trust, and benefit.

"There you have it in five easy pieces. Simple, isn't it?"

"I understand, Perry." The man then shared a story. "Recently we changed our health insurance provider largely over a matter of values and trust. Our prior health-care provider questioned, delayed, and negotiated every claim. This tactic created distrust. We pay big dollars for medical coverage as an employee benefit. All we got were complaints time and time again. Our people thought we had sold them out.

"Our new health-care provider trusts the patient-doctor relationship to make prudent medical and financial decisions. They see themselves as players on the health-care team. The premium payment for the new carrier costs a little more; yet the savings in goodwill and productivity has been well worth it. Trust pays in this case."

"Great example," applauded Perry. "Values *do* influence the customer."

The men finished their meal. Checking his watch, the man anxiously announced, "I'm sorry, but in five minutes I have to leave for an executive team meeting about our largest customer. Perry, in the short time remaining, help me determine my values."

"I can't do that," Perry said calmly. "I can only offer you a method. At least you can work on them some other time. Okay?"

"Deal," the man agreed. He got his pen and paper ready.

"First," Perry began, "write down the names of at least five men and women whom you admire. Next, write down their most admirable personal characteristics. You're making a list, so write freely.

"Next, make another list and record the qualities you most and least admire about yourself. Write next to each of the negative qualities its opposite, or positive, quality. Now you have a list of positive qualities in others and yourself that you admire.

"Pick ten qualities you would like to advance or increase in your life and organization. You now have the raw materials to fashion a set of values. Ta-da!"

"Wow! That's helpful. Thanks!" Checking his watch, the man said, "Perry, I'm sorry, I've got to run." He paid the bill.

## A CONFIDENCE

While waiting for his change, the man leaned close to Perry, a long-trusted confidant, and quietly divulged, "Confidentially, the business is shaky. The owner and president of GEOMay Company, our largest customer, called a meeting about our contract. We're not performing well. Clearly, he's unhappy. We'll lose the business if we don't turn things around. Lots of people could lose their jobs, including me. I'm sick about it. They've been a major customer for decades. It's almost a sure bet we'll lose their business when the contract expires in six months.

"I've scheduled an executive team planning session to review the account. We're going to work on a new contract with hopes of keeping at least part of the business. Pardon me while I dash." The waiter handed the man his change.

Perry's departing advice was "Expect the best! Remember to put into practice what you've been learning about the On-Purpose Business."

They shook hands, and the man left for his office. Perry's final words rang in his ears. He thought about the upcoming meeting. This was certainly an opportune time to put into practice what he had learned . . . on-purpose.

# THE MEETING

▼

*Behind every success,*
*there must be a purpose.*

**Albert E. N. Grey**
*The Common Denominator of Success*

The man anticipated that the executive team meeting would be a challenge. The twenty-five-year relationship with the GEOMay Company was at risk, and so was the company's future.

The man opened the meeting and asked Carter P. Akounz, vice president of finance, to give a financial perspective. Carter reported the facts with an unemotional, detached voice. "GEOMay represents 35 percent of our sales and 30 percent of our net profits. Couple this with their contribution to overhead, and the loss of this account would be devastating."

Sam Cellars, the vice president of sales and marketing, chimed in. "The GEOMay commissions are similar to base pay for many of my folks. Losing the account will cost me sales and sales reps. My best people will jump ship to competitors. They'll take this relationship and others with them. Try recruiting reps when your ship is sinking. Do you know how hard that is?

"We need to compete better on price; at least then we might keep a share of the business. Our manufacturing costs are killing us, and our quality has slid—"

"Hold it there—that's a cheap shot," said Pat Squires, vice president of operations. Pat was a tough, no-nonsense woman with a strong will and a firm grip. "I'm not the fall guy because your sales force can't bring us a complete order. Do you realize that after all your 'training,' your reps still can't fill out a simple order form? To top it off, they change the orders daily. Your reps kill my costs, my performance ratings, and my bonus, buster."

"My people," Sam defended, "are responding to customers. The customer is always right, and we have to help them."

Winfry Harpo was the VP of human resources and a peacemaker. Having risen through the ranks as a training and development specialist, she could usually be counted on to bring order and harmony. She looked at the man and said, "Good luck with this fight."

Pat retorted to Sam, "Hey, I'm busting my tail to serve the customers. Do you know how many rush jobs I did for your sales reps last week alone? Ten! Those disruptions destroy production runs, quality, and budgets. Do I get thanked? No way. From now on your sales guys can just stick it . . ."

"STOP! I've heard enough," the man officiated. "This is getting us nowhere. As we argue over the color to paint the lunch room, the building is burning down around us."

The room grew silent.

"Let's face it. We're all responsible. If we can't get it right between us, then it's no wonder we can't do it right for GEO-May. Imagine how our smaller accounts must feel.

"We're in deep trouble. We have a responsibility to tend to here. The stakes are very high for this company and its employees and affected families, not to mention us. Big layoffs or closing this business will rock this work force and community.

"This business will not go belly-up on my watch without a fight. And the fight won't be from within. We're all responsible for this business."

Next, the man directed, "Call your assistants and clear your calendars for the rest of today and tomorrow. Nothing is more important than this. We're not coming out of this room until we have a plan to rebuild this company and a strategy to keep the GEOMay contract."

Each contacted his or her assistant. With their calendars now available the executives reconvened.

## THE BEGINNING

"Let me share a few things I've learned recently." From this fiery start, the man explained each Pillar of the On-Purpose Business. He was determined to get the hearts, heads, and hands of this team aligned to a single unifying purpose.

"Why does this company exist?" he asked.

They came up with twenty-four reasons. Using the tournament method, they advanced to a meaningful purpose of the organization. It read, "Our company exists to serve by shedding light."

"Shedding Light" carried meaningful nuances, such as illuminating darkness and dispelling confusion; it was a source of answers. The concept of shedding light meant they could lighten the load for others by making things and situations more manageable. It also implied a sense of shining and sharing joy and good cheer, as well as offering an adaptability and flexibility that enabled them to serve in a variety of ways.

A unifying vision for the company naturally emerged. Someone brought up the image of an old-time lamplighter. In the days before electric streetlights, lamplighters brought safety, security, and commerce to unlit areas. Street lamps offered a constant presence to guide, direct, and warn.

The purpose and vision of the company would be lived through the following missions:

1. Development of People
2. Communications
3. Products and Services
4. Community Involvement

They wrote several values that they considered essential to integrity. The first was truthfulness. They determined that they must always be shedding light on truth.

The second value was personal integrity, or living true to self.

A third value was their responsibility as citizens of the community. Never before had they realized the impact of their work on so many lives.

The man asked each person to share what excited him or her about the purpose statement. This was a first pass at establishing the Purpose Principle.

They tapped into the Tingle factor. The business had awesome potential. They felt like they were the founders of the business instead of the curators. The opportunity to serve all the stakeholders — the community, customers, shareholders, employees, and themselves — was in their hands.

Their highly charged session was productive. With renewed energy and cohesiveness, they had lightened their agenda by focusing on the vital few rather than the diffusing many. They had established a purpose and plan for the business. By borrowing from the best of the past and incorporating the best of the present, they had designed an exciting future.

The evening grew late. The man made a bold move when he said at last, "Thank you. Today has been great. We've re-created this company. Now I have one final request. I want job resignations from all of you."

Their mouths dropped open in utter disbelief. He motioned with his hand for them to listen. "Tomorrow morning at eight, I'm re-hiring. I have to know where each of you stands with this new company. If this doesn't feel right, then I will accept your resignation.

"I promise I'll provide outplacement and continue your salary until you land another job. On the other hand, if this little adventure excites you, then show up tomorrow morning at eight. From then on, 100 percent of your focus and commitment is required. No more discussions tonight. We'll reconvene at eight o'clock.

"Thanks for one of the greatest days of my career and for all your hard work. Now go home and sleep on this."

They adjourned at 9:30 P.M. It was a job well done.

## DAY ONE DONE

As the man stayed behind to clean up pizza boxes from dinner, he reflected on the events of the day. In the beginning, each person had a different understanding of the purpose of the business. At one point Pat Squires had observed, "It's no wonder we're always arguing. We've never talked like this before. We never shared a common purpose. I didn't really understand the big picture of business, let alone this business, before today. We're in bad shape."

Carter admitted, "After thirty-plus years as 'just the numbers guy,' the On-Purpose Business perspective opened my eyes. I've naively neglected my business responsibilities. I'm sorry, team."

The executive team had accomplished more in a day than they had in years. Most important of all, a team spirit of optimism finally bound them together as never before.

Tomorrow, the matter at hand was the GEOMay relationship and contract with this "new company." Shoving the pizza boxes into a large trash can and shutting off the lights, the man wondered, *Who's going to show up tomorrow morning?*

126

# 16

# STARTING OVER

▼

*Men and women should
cooperate to study and solve their
problems without envy or
personal ambition and find their
reward in a handsome aggregate
result in which their touch can be
felt but from which their grasp
is absent.*

**Newton Baker (1871–1937)**
*US Secretary of War under President Woodrow Wilson*

The man was encouraged to see each of the leadership team in the office early. Excited to make progress, the meeting began at 7:30 a.m., thirty minutes early. Without exception, each person applied for a "new" job. With *their* on-purpose business still in creation, the team eagerly anticipated the challenges of the GEOMay Company relationship. A positive energy charged the room.

The man smiled and spoke, "Yesterday, for the first time, I felt like I really got to know each of you. I found out what excites you, what matters to you. We're now a phoenix rising from our own ashes." Heads nodded around the room.

The man posed the purpose question, "How can we serve GEOMay by 'shedding light?'"

Sam said, "Last night my head was spinning with ideas and answers to problems that have dogged us for years. With a few marketing enhancements we can position ourselves to rocket into industry leadership once again. Greatness remains in this business. Before yesterday, no one wanted my ideas." Sam was a salesman at heart. It was understandable that he talked with such enthusiasm.

The surprise was Carter, old Mr. Steady, with the company for twenty years. Prior to that, he had been with a public accounting firm. This morning Carter's typically monotone voice bubbled. "About four this morning, I was lying in bed wide awake. We've been in a rut for so long, I had forgotten how to think. That *Think Inc!* jolted me — oxygen to my brain.

"I've got some ideas about pricing. I came in very early this morning and carefully reread the GEOMay contract. There's an incentive bonus we've never met. I know a way we can offer some competitive pricing for GEOMay that can actually save us some costs, ease the wide swings in sales, and enable us to earn the incentive bonus.

"In turn, it creates a more manageable flow in Pat's operations. The disruptive special handling on orders can be minimized. That will keep Pat's costs from spiraling uncontrollably and get her budget in line."

Winfry corrected, "Those aren't Pat's costs and budget. They're *ours!*" Everyone smiled at Winfry's insight.

Pat added, "I love it! Carter, let's explore your ideas right away." Then, turning to Sam, Pat continued, "Actually, Sam, I thought we might work together to create a more competitive package for our customers and especially the GEOMay Company. We'll use the Service Model. There are incredibly talented people working with me. Real lamplighters, if you know what I mean." She winked at the man. "Sam, involve us earlier in the sales process, and we can work miracles if given the chance." Sam smiled with delight.

Winfry offered, "I'll pull together a series of short training programs over the next few days to bring others up to speed on the Pillars of the On-Purpose Business. Let's record an introductory cassette of our purpose and plan so people can listen and learn in their cars. We can spread the excitement throughout the company. . . . Hey, coach," she said, looking at the man, "give me an hour to interview you for this tape." The man agreed.

He sat in stunned wonder. Having tapped into the power of purpose, he realized he mostly just needed to get out of the way. The executive team was now really a team. No longer were they petty defenders of their respective corporate turf. The light switch of purpose was turned on. Each person was shedding light on a situation that had been dark for years. Each person was thinking like a businessperson instead of a narrow-minded functional specialist. It was unlike anything he had ever experienced.

The balance of the morning was spent in hammering out a Service Model approach for GEOMay. If the GEOMay contract was practically lost anyway, then they had everything to gain. By acknowledging their obvious weaknesses they could address them and turn their failings to strengths.

Over the next week they worked out a new proposal in anticipation of the meeting with George F. May III, grandson of the founder of GEOMay Company. The business was infected with being on-purpose. Creative energy and attitudes mobilized everyone. With Winfry's help, the mini-training sessions on the Pillars were offered. The cassette was a hit! "On-PurposeTalk" was heard in hallways, on desktops and workbenches. The purpose, vision, missions, and values statements guided the people with clarity and resolve. Individual confidence and mutual trust grew with each passing day. Corporate renewal followed on the heels of personal transformations. The Tingle was electrifying.

## THE MOMENT OF TRUTH

The day of the GEOMay meeting came at last. A dignified George F. May III and several key executives arrived. George agreed to give the team thirty minutes for a presentation. He said he would listen, although his agenda was to inform.

The presentation followed a simple five-step "shedding light" process. First, they did the unthinkable in business. They admitted their known mistakes, asked for forgiveness of their poor performance, and accepted full responsibility. Next, they shed light on the problems as best they could from GEOMay's perspective. Then they shed light on the fundamental changes of being an on-purpose business. Step four was to provide a schedule for implementing the new plans. Step five was a written promise to perform, signed by every member of the executive team and hundreds of representatives from throughout the ranks of the business. It all made a dramatic impression on George.

At this point in the presentation, the man took a bold move. Holding up the existing contract, he stated, "Almost six months remain on this contract. George, we've known each other a long time, and you know I'm a man of my word. Here's the deal. I'll tear up this contract right now if you want. We'll end it right here and now with no strings attached. Of course, we'll carry you through until you shift to another vendor. For all intents and purposes, the contract in my hand is with a company that no longer exists.

"Ours is a new company," the man declared proudly. He panned his hand toward the vice presidents as icons of the new company. He looked George directly in the eye and said, "We want a new contract with GEOMay Company. Our company is about 'Shedding Light.' We've prepared a new contract, and with your permission let's forge a new relationship between our two companies. May I review it with you?"

George cautiously said, "Proceed."

The team laid out the Service Model designed just for GEOMay. It was revolutionary in the industry: faster deliveries, a tiered pricing schedule, and dedicated customer service.

George, however, had his doubts. "Why should I believe you can do this after the years of poor performance you've just admitted?"

The man responded, "George, there's only one reason. The men and women in this room and in this company give you our word. We'll perform as promised. We're so confident we can perform on this contract that I'll add a handwritten addendum. With a thirty-day written notice, we're gone. It's that easy. We want you raving about us rather than raging at us.

"Successful pilot programs are underway right now. Glitches are bound to happen; yet we're committed to learning and improving over the remaining six months on the old contract."

Moving from the defensive to the offensive, the man asked the question. "So, George, do I tear up this old contract? Do you walk or do you stay to redefine a new, improved relationship? We want to be a lamplighter for your company. What's your decision?"

The moment of truth had arrived. The man felt the tension, yet he remained confident. He knew this proposed contract would be hard for George to decline. Also, he knew his company and people were on the verge of a breakthrough. If George wouldn't buy it, then others would. The GEOMay contract enabled an orderly progression to the changeover. In that regard it was important.

George was jotting notes. Without raising his head, he peered over his Ben Franklin half-framed glasses and coldly stated, "My grandfather taught me to shoot straight with people. That's what I'm doing. After all, you employ many people in this community and others; families depend on you for a paycheck. So out of respect for the years we've worked together . . . I'm here to inform you ahead of time that we will not be renewing the contract. I wanted you to be warned so you could begin making alternative arrangements. Today, I end doing business with your company. Tear up that contract."

The man felt his heart sink. The other team members gasped. They had miscalculated. Apparently, the damage was too deep for a reversal.

Had the man been a fool to think they could salvage this relationship? If George couldn't see the logic and strength of this proposal, would others? Was bankruptcy protection their last alternative? The reality of losing the GEOMay account hit hard.

Having invested so much of himself the past week in the possibilities of success, he hadn't prepared himself for a different outcome. With George and everyone else watching, he began tearing up the contract. With each shred, his hurt turned to a resolve to excel.

George dispassionately watched the ritual death of the relationship. When the man finished, George broke the dead silence. "I wondered if you really would tear up that contract."

George's countenance changed. A smile broke from the corner of his mouth. "I'm fascinated with the thirty minutes of magic you all have presented. You took my reasons for terminating this contract and addressed them all. It's like you read my mind. In fact, you exceeded what I thought was possible. You've shown some creativity I didn't think existed in this company. I'm impressed.

"I'll engage your *new* company. Take the six months remaining under the old contract to get your act together. Deliver as promised, and I'll renew. If you don't make it right—we're gone. You've been warned. Do we have an understanding?"

"Yes! We *will* perform," the man pledged. His spirits soared. He looked around the room to the team. Their faces shone with pride.

George continued, "I like the leadership and fresh thinking you're providing since Fred's retirement. There's a strong and positive attitude here. I foresee a bright future . . . assuming you perform as promised."

Now looking at the man, George added, "I'm imposing one condition. You proposed a stronger alliance between our businesses. I agree. Let's get our people working together as soon as possible. Our people need to be a part of putting together that, uh . . . Service Model, I think you called it." Then turning to one of the executives accompanying him, George said, "Let's work with these good people to partner in their success."

George stood and shook hands with the man, Winfry, Carter, Sam, and Pat. After George's departure, the team gave each other high fives and hugs to celebrate. They had triumphed and averted the imminent disaster.

Massive work lay ahead. Yet, they could proceed with newfound confidence in a purpose, plan, process, and in people and performance aligned to serve their customers. It tingled.

For the first time, they had done a major deal without the Old Man. This was their deal. The man felt great about the company and the new milestone. He wondered to himself, *Now, how in the world do we sustain this? I've never done anything like this before. This is why Pillar Four, the Manner of the On-Purpose Business, is important.*

The time was right to see Hal again. In the midst of his largest career victory, he knew he was still short one Pillar — the Manner.

# 17

# THE ON-PURPOSE PALETTE

▼

*Today, systems thinking is needed more than ever because we are becoming overwhelmed by complexity. . . . Organizations break down, despite individual brilliance and innovative products, because they are unable to pull their diverse functions and talents into a productive whole.*

**Peter M. Senge**
*The Fifth Discipline*

Finding his way to the familiar park bench, the man sat and waited for Hal. He appeared on a path carrying a shovel and an empty watering can.

The men shook hands. Hal welcomed the man: "Good to see you. I brought my shovel in case that little old stick doesn't garner your attention anymore," Hal teased.

"Hal, it's remarkable." The man recounted the story of the GEOMay contract. Smiling from ear to ear, Hal listened and watched the man's command performance. "The three Pillars we've used so far are awesome. We devised a memory jogger to help use the Pillars. We call it the On-Purpose Palette."

"Tell me about it," Hal requested.

"Artists use a palette to hold and mix colors so they can create what they want. That's what the Palette does for us. Each Pillar is assigned a primary color. The Purpose Principle is red for the heart. *Think Inc!* we labeled blue because it deals with the mind's eye and blue-sky thinking—and my daughter's eyes are blue. The Service Model is the yellow Pillar because we use it day to day, and the yellow sun symbolizes a day."

Hal's eyes twinkled. "I love it! Go on."

The man offered, "By mixing the three primary colors of red, blue, and yellow, any color can be created. We see challenges or opportunities as having three perspectives. Once each perspective is discussed, we mix the colors to fit the picture. This enables us to deal systematically with the full spectrum of issues."

"For example?" Hal invited.

"For example . . ."—the man was thinking—"to increase sales. What's the challenge? Before the Palette, we would try promotions, advertising, sales incentives, and so forth. They're all short-term performance enhancers but not necessarily connected to a long-term approach. We now have a systematic way to approach a sales increase. Here's what we do now.

"RED: Using the Purpose Principle, we evaluate sales from a personal and organizational perspective. *On the organizational side*: Have we clearly articulated the purpose of the organization so the sales team can align with it? Perhaps the purpose of the organization is moving off-purpose and our customers sense it before we do. How are our Technical and Tingle factors aligning? *On the personal side*: Do people feel a sense of belonging and personal importance? Is a salesperson's purpose aligned with the purpose of the organization? In other words, is the Tingle high or low? Is Technical training needed?"

Hal nodded his head. "The seeds to a good answer are often found in the right questions."

"Now, there's the truth," the man corroborated.

"BLUE: With *Think Inc!*" the man continued, "we evaluate our mindset relative to sales. Are we thinking like owners and presidents? Have we considered long and short-term effects? Do we understand the profit-and-loss potential? Are responsibility and authority connected? What are the personal, professional, and corporate risks and rewards? Are they appropriate for the people involved? Has some Stink Inc. or blaming crept into our midst?

"YELLOW: the Service Model. What needs to happen at the front line? What are our customers saying? Do we have structural problems within the Service Model? Are the linkages and relative order from level to level properly aligned? Have we changed the Plan yet not put in motion the appropriate changes at the Performance level and points in between? Have we made an inadvertent change at the Performance level that isn't supported by the lower levels or vice versa? Are we communicating effectively? Have we altered or departed from our values?

"Using the Palette, we are a company of business-people. From the mail room to the board room, everyone is engaged in learning and improving the business because it's as easy as remembering the three primary colors."

Hal commented, "The Palette is ingenious. With all those On-Purpose Businesspersons, I predict great things for your business. Well done!"

"Thanks. I'm ready to move on to Pillar Four — 'Doing More of What You Do Best More Profitably.' Will you help?" asked the man.

Hal nodded and then posed a question. "Using your Palette, what color is Pillar Four?"

The man snapped his head back. "I don't know."

"Remember that the Manner of the On-Purpose Business embodies the other Pillars. May I suggest white as the color for Pillar Four? If you shine a white light through a prism, a rainbow emerges. White light holds it all."

"Hal," the man said, "I love it! What a phenomenal observation. Thanks for 'shedding light' on that."

"Consider it my contribution. I see lots of rainbows spraying water in the sunlight. Now, let's get you to your next On-Purpose Partner. See John Harold. I believe you know each other?"

"Yes, we do," said the man, grimacing. He thought, *Of all the people, why John Harold?* John was the pastor of a church. *What can a pastor know about building a business? Becoming an On-Purpose Business sure stretches my comfort zone.*

Hal closed with, "Our lessons are complete. Let's visit again, though."

The man added his appreciation. "Thanks for helping

me. One last thing: I'm glad you didn't need that shovel today!" With that, Hal faked a strike with the shovel. The two men laughed and shared a parting hug.

# 18

# MATTERS OF MANNER

▼

*Simple, clear purpose and*
*principles give rise to complex*
*and intelligent behavior. Complex*
*rules and regulations give rise to*
*simple and stupid behavior.*

**Dee Hock**
*Founder and CEO Emeritus of Visa International*

It was late in the afternoon. The man headed to the church office to meet John Harold. Passing by the sanctuary door, he heard a children's choir practicing. Their voices carried an angelic and peaceful sound. Pausing by the open door, he listened and breathed in the music. The purity drew him into a calm reflection.

Turning from the door, his mind returned to his upcoming appointment. What this meeting had to do with his business, he didn't know. He thought, *I'm a businessman, a pragmatist, someone who needs proof. As far as I know, the whole world is just one big accident that keeps fermenting like witches' brew.* Matters of faith had always disturbed him. He had never come to terms with the concept of God.

The man and Pastor John Harold were acquainted from a previous visit. John had a knack for urging him to consider spiritual matters. That's why the man wasn't looking forward to this meeting.

"Faith," the man would say to his wife, "is a personal matter. I try to be a good person. That's what really counts." And then he would think of a question like *Does God exist?* It was confusing.

Stepping inside the church office, the man spied John Harold near the receptionist's desk. They immediately greeted each other. At their prior meeting, John had worn a madras shirt without a clerical collar. He had humorously described himself as being "undercover." Today, he wore a black shirt with a white clerical collar.

The man joked, "I see you're in battle dress today! Are you going to 'save' me? Maybe I should come back when it's safe."

The pastor smiled. "Stay! Salvation is already a done deal. Want me to explain it to you?"

The man cowered away in mock fear.

"Stay anyway," the minister encouraged. His eyes narrowed and he coyly added, "Otherwise, how will you learn about Pillar Four?"

"Deal! Now you're talking," the businessman replied. "I want to learn about the Manner."

John, pretending to strike an auctioneer's gavel, said, "Sold on Pillar Four!" Then placing his left arm around the man's shoulder, John chuckled, "You asked for that." The man agreed.

"Let's go to my office and talk about the Manner of the On-Purpose Church—oops, I mean the On-Purpose Business. Same Manner, just a different setting."

After the two had seated themselves on comfortable chairs in the pastor's office, John commented, "Pillar Four saved me from major burnout. I learned to let go of what I don't do best and leave it to someone else who does do it best. Being on-purpose is freeing and fun.

"Many of my peers try to do it all and be 'perfect' instead of being themselves. The diverse challenges of this work can lead to collapse. Sadly, clergy burnout and divorce are uncommonly high. When our personal setbacks come, they are so public that we damage the very cause we're trying to advance. Being on-purpose is vital for maintaining a healthy life perspective, especially for leaders with a watching public."

"Sounds a lot like my job as president of the company," the man said. "My waking hours are consumed with work. I guess being a pastor *is* like running a business."

John nodded in agreement. "That's why we must be true to our purpose. It's easy to become seduced by our public. Pillar Four helps us be at peace and focused on who we are and aren't. Then we act accordingly."

"Great," the man said with enthusiasm. "Why is Pillar Four known as the Manner?"

"There are several reasons," John explained. "Manners are learned choices and conduct. Good manners elevate us from a natural state into a refined state. Pillar Four is all about choice. We constantly choose to act, think, behave, and organize by Doing More of What You Do Best More Profitably at the personal and organizational levels."

"You slipped in some new stuff: 'at the personal and organizational levels.' What's up with this?"

"The church is not the building, it's the people," John explained. Moving to the edge of his chair, he added, "The same is true of any business or organization. As the people grow, so grows the organization. We leaders must be growing because we influence the entire organization.

"Let's put it in terms of a family. A well-mannered father will likely pass fine manners on to his children. Mastery of manners is an important life attribute."

"Manners matter," the man agreed. "Manners are also 100 percent my choice, once I have awareness. There are very few other places in business or life where I can say that."

"Correct!" John confirmed. "Do you see why a manner is a powerful Pillar for one's life, career, and business?" The man nodded his head.

John resumed, "If you have no manner upon which to direct your life or business, then by which manner are you running it?"

"Without a chosen manner, I guess I choose whatever seems right at the time," ventured the man.

"And the consequences of your situational conduct are . . . ?" John led him.

"Chaos. There's no consistency. I'm here, I'm there. One day it's this decision, the next day it's another. I'm confused, and those around me are confused."

John continued, "Yes. Manners simplify living and life. They help integrate, synthesize, and align a person's heart, head, and hands. They do the same collectively for an organization. A manner is a rule of life that helps you stay on-purpose in your new way of life or business."

"I don't get it," the man commented.

"I realize the Bible isn't a reference for your life," John said, pausing to smile before he continued, "and yet, there's a short story from the Bible that clearly illustrates the point. May I tell you a Bible story?"

"Hey, I'm here to learn," the man replied. "Go ahead, use whatever book you want if it helps me learn."

# 19

# THE GREAT MANNER

▼

*I love being on-purpose. I'm saying no to increasingly better opportunities and saying yes more frequently to the best opportunities.*

**Paul G. Anthes**
*President, Financial Advisory Corporation*

John Harold was once the chief financial officer (CFO) of a successful privately owned company. Following a call into the ministry in his late thirties, he changed careers. He related especially well to business people and their day-to-day challenges, pressures, and temptations because he was once in the thick of the business world.

"So tell me the Bible story," invited the man, "so I can understand this Manner stuff."

John smiled and thought, *He's just like I was—all business. Get the deal done; do the transaction and move on to the next. Avoid getting too deep.*

John began, "You'll need some background to appreciate the story. Have you heard of the Ten Commandments?"

"Heard of them, of course," the man replied. "I even saw the movie."

"Good," said the pastor. "Now let me set a later scene. One day more than a thousand years after Moses brought the commandments down from the mountain, the chief priests and Pharisees were questioning Jesus about His teaching 'credentials.' These powerful men were keepers of the Jewish law, rules, and traditions. Jesus' radical teachings had threatened their authority, position, and power. So the Pharisees set a trap, hoping to entangle Jesus with His own words.

"One of the Pharisees, a lawyer and religious scholar, ambushed Him by asking, 'Teacher, which is the greatest commandment in the Law?'"

The man asked, "How's that a trick question?"

"Look at Jesus' three possible responses," the pastor explained. "He could have given no response, or chosen one of the commandments, or responded that all the laws are equal.

"The entrapment was this: The "correct" response, according to the Pharisees, was that all commandments were from God through Moses, and therefore all are equal. If Jesus answered this way, He would show that He was a traditionalist and under their authority. They could then readily denounce His other teachings.

"If Jesus responded that one law was above the others, He would be deemed a heretic, and His blasphemy would be a punishable offense.

"Finally, if He chose not to respond, He would be deemed a novice with no authority."

Listening intently, the man said, "Fascinating—more like prime-time TV than the Bible." A thought flashed in his mind: *Can this ancient story actually have practical application today?* Now up on the edge of his chair, he demanded, "So, what was His answer?"

John Harold paused, then said, "Jesus replied, 'Love the Lord your God with all your heart and with all your soul and with all your mind. This is the first and greatest commandment. And the second is like it: Love your neighbor as yourself. All the Law and the Prophets hang on these two commandments.'"

"Bold choice," said the man with admiration. "He took the heretic response. A guy with guts. How'd our boys the Pharisees take it?"

"As you might expect," John replied, "most branded Him a heretic; a few were convicted by the truth. That's the irony. The Pharisees were so intent on the letter of the law that they were blind to Christ's profound message of the spirit of the law being grounded in love, not rules. He distilled complex and even contradictory teachings, laws, traditions, rules, and customs into a simple *manner* of living. In doing so, He reformed the faith. His brilliant response is known as the Great Commandment."

"Inspiring story! Is that really in the Bible?" the man questioned. "Or did you make that up for me?"

John laughed. "Look at the book of Matthew in the twenty-second chapter, verses thirty-four to forty. By the way, that's in the New Testament, the books toward the back," he teased. "You'll find many profound and practical truths in the Bible. Read it sometime."

Amused, the pastor continued, "You are so much like I was years ago. It's amazing."

"What do you mean?"

"Your apprehension of the Bible and organized religion is understandable. I know how you feel. I felt the same way. I, too, had preconceived notions on faith, God, Jesus, and other spiritual matters clouded by dogma. My views were fashioned from my childhood and teenage experiences.

"Instead of writing it all off, why don't you evaluate it as an adult? Promise me we'll get together one day and really talk out the spiritual foundation of life." Sliding into his old business terminology, the on-purpose pastor extended his hand. "Deal?"

"You're good," said the man, accepting John's hand. "You weren't a CFO, you were a VP of sales and marketing. I'll shake on it and listen to your pitch someday.

"But today, let's get back to the Manner, please."


PILLAR FOUR

"We already are," John replied. "The Manner is a simplifying operational mantra that equips people to right themselves regardless of the situation, dilemma, or conflict. Through the Great Commandment, Jesus was shedding light on all the teachings, laws, traditions, rules, and customs, especially the Ten Commandments. In essence, if you live according to this one manner, everything else will take care of itself."

The man's ears perked up. He stopped John and said, "You said 'shedding light.' That's the purpose statement for my company. Amazing that you would use those words."

The pastor responded, What's even more remarkable is Jesus said, 'I am the "light" of the world.' Your purpose statement has evangelical implications.

The man rolled his eyes, crossed his arms, and turned in his chair as he said, "Gimme a break. Tell me about the Manner."

John chuckled and continued, "The Manner of the On-Purpose Business is 'Doing More of What You Do Best More Profitably.' We'll break it into thirds.

"Let's start with the center third, 'What You Do Best.' When you're on-purpose, you have a monopoly. It's excellence relative to self. When you're at your best, then meaning, fulfillment, and performance are sure to follow."

The man nodded.

John resumed, "The lead third, 'Doing More,' relates to the Service Model, or Pillar Three. Using the Service Model we can make "what we do best" happen with greater regularity.

"The final third of the statement is 'More Profitably.' I'm using *profit* to mean adding value in its broadest sense. We're talking value relative to community as well as personal and financial aspects. Social profit exists in smiles, hugs, happiness, trust, and positive feelings. Financial profit is the excess of revenues after expenses and is one of many measures rather than the only measure of profit.

Get that distinction! We business types tend to lock in on financial profit exclusively. Recall that the Service Model is designed to create value adding at the front line."

The man smiled. "I like it. 'Doing More of What You Do Best More Profitably' is a surefire road to success. I've watched many businesses, including mine, try to do more of what we don't do best, only to be unprofitable — in terms of morale and finances. It's disastrous."

The pastor added, "What you've just described is the malady that's menacing lots of leaders today. We try to be all things to all people.

"In the church we carry the extra burden of our work being 'ministry.' Serving is never-ending, so where can one draw the line? Here at this church, we believe in the whole body of Christ at work, and we are but one member of a larger body. We focus on our unique purpose and refer many needs to other churches and ministries. Businesses must likewise fight the temptation of trying to be all things to all customers."

## THE ON-PURPOSE CHURCH

"I'm curious about something," said the man. "What's the purpose statement for this church?"

"'Showing The Way.' The longer version is 'To the glory of God, we exist to serve by Showing The Way.'"

"The way to where?" the man inquired.

"Since you asked," said John with a smile, "the way to God. And Christ is that Way. Each word in our purpose statement packs a punch. 'Showing' means demonstrating, revealing, leading, and giving. 'Way' is a means, passage, and manner. '*The* Way' means there is only one way. So when we put it all together, we are 'Showing The

Way' every day in every action we take."

"For instance?" the man asked.

"My relationship with you is an example," John stated. "I show The Way to you when I invite you to deepen your spiritual perspective." John scratched his head. "Funny thing is, you'll listen to me on business matters, but not on what I do best . . . faith. Odd, isn't it?"

The man shrugged his shoulders and teased, "Hey, you can lead a horse to water, but you can't make him drink—right? Anyway, you've been terrific thus far. I hate to ruin a friendship by discussing religion."

"You're incorrigible," laughed the pastor.

"Sorry," the man apologized. "It's just that religion isn't really for me."

"Me either," John agreed.

"Hey, that's your specialty—what you do best," protested the man.

John chuckled and calmly replied, "My specialty is 'Showing the Way.' I have the road map. I've made the wrong turns and hit the dead ends. I've been there. I'm offering to show you the Way."

"Where am I?" prompted the man.

"You're close."

"Close to where?" the man questioned.

John reassured, "Close to wholeness, peace, contentment . . . close to being on-purpose, of course. In the church we talk of being in God's will. In laypeople's language that's being on-purpose. Remember the light switch? You're either off- or on-purpose . . . out of or in God's will."

"Why do you say that about me?" questioned the man.

"Your search is of a spiritual nature. The business is just a platform that reveals your needs. Your life has a built-in design. And you have a free will to accept or reject it. Once you embrace it rather than run from it, then God can go to work in your life. And God, well, He's got some serious resources," joked the pastor. "And He forgives debts!"

This conversation was paradoxical for the man. His head was spinning. John's words disturbed yet comforted him. The man resisted this line of conversation, yet he had invited it. He came to talk business, not about his spiritual life. Yet both were somehow linked.

He brought the talk back within his comfort zone by asking, "How do I apply this to my business?"

"As the leader of the company goes, so goes the business. Your best and worst attributes are amplified throughout the organization. Your position, like mine, carries high visibility and responsibility. There's no escaping your personal influence on the health and well-being of any organization you lead, whether it's a business, church, or family."

"So this all comes back to aligning your heart, head, and hands, doesn't it?"

"Yes! Let's tie it all together." John borrowed the man's journal and sketched out a table. "Take a look."

## Pillar Four: THE MANNER

| Doing More of . . . | What You Do Best . . . | More Profitably |
|---|---|---|
| Hands | Heart | Head |
| Pillar Three | Pillar One | Pillar Two |
| Service Model | Purpose Principle | *Think Inc!* |
| Yellow | Red | Blue |

The man looked at the chart and added the Palette colors. He briefly explained the Palette to the pastor. The man commented, "The Manner really is like the Great Commandment. The first three Pillars *are* contained in the Manner."

"You've got it! Now live it!" John exclaimed with a smile.

## AWESOME RESPONSIBILITY

Their time together had been brief, yet the pastor's touch was indelibly imprinted on the man. Walking to his car, he contemplated, *No matter where I turn, the influence of my purpose on the lives of others keeps arising. John was right; I can't avoid it. I never sensed the high leverage my purpose has on the ultimate performance of the organization. It's an awesome responsibility.*

Turning the key in the ignition, he cranked up his car and pulled out of the church parking lot. As he did, his cellular phone rang. He answered, "Hello."

"Hi! Jackie said I might catch you in your car." It was the professor.

"Hi, Professor! Great to hear from you. So what's the purpose of your call?" asked the man, laughing at turning around the professor's usual question to him.

"I've created a monster," laughed the professor. "Bob Scott and I talked. We've arranged for you to meet Eric Jeffries tomorrow morning at eight. Jackie said your calendar is open most of the day, and she rearranged some morning meetings so you're free all day.

"Pardon my boldness with your day. This is important. Eric leaves for Europe on a business trip in two days. Before he leaves, you two need to meet. By the way, dress comfortably."

"I'll be there." The man got the directions to Eric's home. When he pulled into his driveway at home, his arrival brought excited expressions from his kids at the front window. He thought, *Wow, I have the same influence in my home as I do at work. Another awesome responsibility. I hope I'm an on-purpose parent.*

Walking into his home, he hugged and kissed his wife and children. After dinner he crashed onto the couch and fell asleep. His wife woke him to come to bed around eleven o'clock. The events of the past few weeks had been exhilaratingly exhausting.

---

# $\boxed{20}$

# THE MICRO-BUSINESS

▼

*I have seen the business that God has given to everyone to be busy with. . . . It is God's gift that all should eat and drink and take pleasure in all their toil.*

**Ecclesiastes 3:10,13, NRSV**

The man awoke feeling refreshed. He threw on casual clothes and grabbed a bagel and some orange juice on the way out the door. Jeans and a sweater were a welcome change from his usual Tom James suit, polished leather shoes, and Windsor-knotted tie.

His trip to see Eric Jeffries routed him through downtown. People jammed the streets on their way to work. Passing between skyscrapers, he was struck that thousands of people worked in these steel and glass enclosures. How many were happy? How many had fulfilling work . . . or lives?

How many were just putting in time from paycheck to paycheck in hopes of some fanciful future life called retirement? How many were actually living their dream or even had any dreams left?

How many had a piece of their soul die every day they entered those buildings? How many knew they even had options?

He thought it would make a fascinating study to survey all the people in one building for the answers to these questions.

Heading his car onto the freeway, he wondered about his friends. These were successful people, from all outward appearances, yet few had real joy in their lives. Life was rigorous rather than vigorous. They faced the numbing daily grind, a legacy of complacency. He related well. Only now he had a new awareness, a sense of possibilities and hope. Perhaps John Harold was right.

The professor said Eric Jeffries operated a business from his home. Guiding his car off the Bethel Street exit, the man followed the directions to Lindermer Avenue, where Eric lived. He stopped at the first two-story home on the right and checked the street numbers: 4-9-7-8.

This was it. After parking his car on the street, he walked to the front porch and rang the doorbell.

Eric Jeffries opened the door and shook the man's hand. "Welcome! C'mon in. We have a few minutes before we leave. Let me show you around." Eric was a tall, well-built man with a large, easy smile, firm handshake, and receding hairline. The home was spacious and well decorated. This was an affluent section of town, and Eric's home tastefully reflected financial success.

"Thanks," said the man. He wasn't sure what to expect. Whatever could he have to discuss with a guy with a home business? It seemed incongruent to be there. Then again, Pam Dimes had taught him plenty.

The man asked, "We're leaving soon? Where are we going?"

"You'll find out," Eric said with a laugh and a wink. "Don't worry. C'mon, let me show you my office."

The two men stepped into a good-sized room with a magnificent view of the distant mountains ablaze with autumn colors. Eric's office was loaded with electronic gadgets and books. "I'm state of the art here, fully automated and nearly paperless," he said. He then swept his hand toward a wall-sized bookcase. "And my books — here's where I choose not to be paperless. I love my books. I have books on personal development, business, parenting, gardening, philosophy, and biographies. Ten pages a day keeps my mind from running astray."

"I like that," the man said with a chuckle. He warmed easily to Eric.

"Pull up a chair," Eric said as he rolled a high-backed chair directly in front of the man. "I imagine you're wondering what you can learn from a guy running a business from his home?"

"As a matter of fact, that's exactly what I was wondering. I admit, however, I've learned more from a gardener than I imagined possible. Why not a guy who works from his home?"

Eric continued, "You're looking at the future. What you see in this office is what is happening with a huge percentage of the working population."

"To work alone at home?" asked the man.

"No. Don't confuse location with the issue. I'm not alone in my business. I have associates throughout the world. We're connected. I'm free to do what I do best more profitably. I want you to see the substance of this, not the form.

"Home businesses reflect the coming economic era of the micro-business in the Age of Purpose. Those of us in home businesses are economic pioneers. We're forging new ways of doing business, of relating and collaborating. The On-Purpose Business is the way of the micro-business."

The man said, "So what?"

"This is the wave of the future. Whether I'm physically located in the home or office is irrelevant. The fact is, there's work to be done. People with creative minds in a collaboration are essential. The ways of business have changed forever. Our minds, bodies, and spirits are liberated from physical location thanks to technology."

"I see. You're proposing each person is an On-Purpose Business, right?"

"Yes, absolutely."

"But what of organizations as we know them today? If we've reduced all service to the level of one person, don't we need some organizing factor?"

"Exactly!" Eric exclaimed.

"Exactly what?"

Eric was excited. "That's what the On-Purpose Business does. It enables a micro-business of one or a company with thousands to share a common structure and method of operation. If a business exists to serve, then the Four Pillars are the four corners needed to successfully build a business."

"And I never thought big business people could learn anything from small business practices admitted the man. The Four Pillars stand true regardless of the size of an organization."

"A micro-business? Tell me more about that," he requested.

"A micro-business is a business of one person. Who are we? We're salespeople and consultants. Some of us are individual distributors for direct-sales and multi-level marketing companies, others are artists and cottage industrialists. We're entrepreneurs. We're salaried employees who *Think Inc!* within the context of a job. Every working person is a micro-business whether he or she acknowledges it or not.

"What are we? We're a fast and flexible work force technologically networked with satellite dishes, cellular phones, E-mail, and groupware. We fiercely guard our independence and cherish collaboration. We're pioneers on the new frontiers of business and the economy. This work style brings us greater personal fulfillment, balance, and relationships. We are on-purpose."

The man folded his arms across his chest with skepticism. "Sounds to me like a bunch of idealistic escapists from corporate America who couldn't get a job and have resorted to this idealistic rationale for being unemployable."

Eric didn't flinch. "On the contrary, we're ultimate realists. We don't seek employment. We want expression of our purpose, a managed life, and a sense of belonging. We have embraced the challenges of our times to make it the best in our lives. Growth and learning are our accepted way of life; only our purpose remains constant."

The man pushed. "What of companies like Bob Scott's? Do you predict the demise of large corporations?"

"No, they're moving our way. Outsourcing is just one of many clues. Companies like Bob's already recruit us to work with them because we work well together. We're part of the team that's housed elsewhere and on call as needed. We're temporary workers with full-time on-purpose positions and multiple clients."

"This *is* the wave of the future," Eric insisted. "It's the ultimate On-Purpose Business in the smallest sense of the word. Micro-business people are highly fluid from project to project, even job to job — not from necessity or weakness, but from choice and strength.

"Wow! I get it!" the man exclaimed.

"The Four Pillars are really universal principles guiding organizational development. It is a whole new way to do business."

The man motioned to the skies with his hand. "This micro-business concept seems way out there. I guess in the virtual workplace we will need a protocol for fast connection and alignment. The On-Purpose Business provides that very standard operating procedure."

Suddenly, Eric's voice emanated from the computer at his desk. "Reminder: You have an On-Purpose Partners Meeting in thirty minutes."

"Thank you," Eric said to the machine. "Turn off reminder." He turned to the man and explained, "Just a voice chip and a software program that help me stay on-purpose."

The computer replied, "Ten-four, good buddy!"

"Let's go," Eric said. They headed out the back door of Eric's home into the garage. There they hopped into Eric's car and were off to the meeting.

# 21

# ON-PURPOSE PARTNERS

▼

*It's simple. . . . We either get used
to thinking about the subtle
process of learning and sharing
knowledge in dispersed, transient
networks, or we perish.*

**Tom Peters**
*The Tom Peters Seminar*

Eric pulled onto the freeway. Peering out the window into the distance, the man contemplated all that was happening. He couldn't help thinking about Fred Taylor. Had Fred seen him gallivanting about town like this, *he* would be dead instead of Fred. The Old Man measured one's commitment to the company by the time logged at the office. Over the past few months it was as if the man were participating in a personal and organizational scavenger hunt. Fred's memory and methods continued to haunt him despite all he had learned, taught, and experienced.

He thought about Eric. *This guy is incredible.* Remembering his proposed study of the downtown office workers, he decided to start the study informally with Eric. If nothing else, it would make for interesting conversation.

Rather directly, he asked, "Are you happy?"

"Positively! I'm on-purpose!" Eric replied.

"So, what's your purpose?" asked the man.

"'Radiating Joy.' My purpose statement is, 'I exist to serve by Radiating Joy.'"

"Well, you certainly are good at that. You're one of the most joyful persons I've ever met."

"Thank you. I wasn't always this way. We TOP Performers encourage each other because most people don't know what to make of us. We're going to this meeting so we can learn and share with other people running On-Purpose Businesses."

"Really? There are more people like you?"

Eric smiled. "Lots more. Even in my micro-business, I face the very same issues you do as president of that monolithic company. The differences between our two companies are tradition, formality, and control."

The man boasted, ". . . and sales."

Eric smiled at the man's subtle attempt at the mine-is-bigger game. He decided to teach the man a lesson. He asked the man, "What kind of sales numbers do you think I do from my house?"

Regretting his childish comment, the man guessed way high. "Two million bucks a year."

"Higher," Eric baited.

The man dug his hole deeper. This time he would really overshoot the sales figure by being absurd. "Five million dollars a year."

"Higher," Eric laughed.

"No way!" sneered the man.

"Way!" Eric smiled unflinchingly.

The man realized Eric was truthful. He doubled his guess. "Ten million."

"Higher" was Eric's now familiar chant.

"Twenty million dollars."

"Higher," Eric encouraged. He was clearly enjoying this little game the man had started, and he was finishing. Finally he lowered the boom. "I'll do fifty-five million dollars this year from that home office. By the way, I'll net more than your company will this year. I've read your quarterly projections; it's been a tough year. In fact, I'll likely give charities more money through my foundation than your company will make."

The man was visibly shaken. "That's impossible," he stammered. "How can you operate a business of that size from one room?"

"By applying the Four Pillars of the On-Purpose Business with others who are doing the same."

"Where are your people?"

"They're all over. My micro-business is really a

macro-business. I have thousands of associates working with me in a variety of functions. We collaborate using the Four Pillars. By doing this I've created an enormous organization. It's duplicable because we all agree on the On-Purpose Business approach. That's how I've built a fifty-five-million-dollar company with a payroll of one. Even my administrative assistant is her own business. Pretty incredible, isn't it?"

"I'll say. Where did you ever come up with these ideas?" asked the man.

"They're from my On-Purpose Partners."

"Your what?" asked the man.

"Napoleon Hill, in his classic book *Think and Grow Rich*, wrote of the importance of a mastermind group. Hill's book was released in 1937. It offered tremendous insights and many valuable principles. Yet, Hill was a product of the Industrial Age, and much of his writing springs from a past era. His writing was about the mind.

"We're centered on the heart. Think of it as a 'master heart' group. We call them On-Purpose Partners Meetings."

## THE ON-PURPOSE PARTNERS

It was one revelation after the next. Eric pulled the car into a parking space next to a suburban hotel. They entered the lobby. After glancing at the meeting room assignments on the color monitor, Eric led the man to a boardroom.

There was a tap on the man's shoulder, and a familiar voice said, "Welcome, friend." It was Perry James, accompanied by Bob Scott. They warmly greeted him. The man was surprised to see their familiar faces.

Perry said, "I'm happy you're here today. This Partners Meeting was founded by Hal Trudy many years ago.

Some begin the process, few commit to it, and fewer still are invited to participate. Others, like your old boss Fred Taylor, never took an interest in learning about the On-Purpose Business.

"We have one rule in Partners Meetings: Anything you hear in this room is confidential. Agreed?"

"Agreed," said the man. He was flattered by this invitation.

Bob graciously introduced the man to each person in the room. He recognized many of them as prominent people in the community.

The man asked, "Is the professor here?"

Bob answered, "No, he attends a Partners Meeting for educators. There are meetings for different professions."

"How many meetings for different professions are there?" the man probed.

"Many. There are Partners Meetings for nonprofit organizations, government, arts and entertainment, sports, churches, homemakers, and others."

"Do the groups ever meet jointly?"

"Absolutely," Bob replied. "Those are more like regional conventions. Everyone is welcome. They're fun. The rich diversity is impressive. We'll talk later—Perry is about to start the meeting."

They sat around the conference table. Each partner gave an update on a variety of personal and professional issues. As one spoke, the others made notes in journals.

The man observed the Pillars come alive before his very eyes. For the next four hours, this board of mutual advisers intensively analyzed, critiqued, focused, and developed one another's personal and professional lives and businesses. Everything was open for discussion.

They dealt with strategic issues, then brainstormed projects, problems, and opportunities. Sometimes they networked to connect each other with resources. Each person had ample time to voice his or her needs. Laughter frequently filled the room.

When the Partners Meeting ended, Eric had to run to another meeting. Bob Scott gave the man a ride to Eric's house to pick up his car. He inquired, "What did you think of our time together today?"

"I was blown away," the man bubbled. "I've never experienced anything like that before. The collective advice, wisdom, and creativity generated an energy unlike any I've ever felt. It was as if an invisible presence were guiding the meeting."

"That Tingle is the presence and power of purpose. You experienced pure service in a community of TOP Businesspersons running TOP Businesses."

Bob continued, "We have two openings in our Partners Meeting. I have the pleasure of inviting you to join us. We've been cultivating you for some time and feel you're ready. Are you interested?"

The man jumped at the opportunity. "Yes, count me in. I'm honored. How in the world do you have two openings? Who in their right mind would leave a group like that?"

Bob grinned. "We're having a 'baby.' Two members of our Partners Meeting are birthing a new one. Their departure is a sign of growth. They've been trained to facilitate the meetings. It's special when we reproduce like cells. It means that more people can deepen their On-Purpose Business practices.

"By the way, the other person who will soon be invited to join is Pam Dimes."

"That's great," said the man, beaming. "Tell me the

details." Bob Scott proceeded to spell out the guidelines and commitments for participation. The ride was a blur for the man. His head spun with excitement.

# 22

# THE INTERVIEW

▼

*"For what shall it profit a man, if
he shall gain the whole world,
and lose his own soul?"*

**Jesus Christ**
*Mark 9:36 (KJV)*

The reporter sat with her pen and paper, furiously scribbling notes. The interview had lasted more than two hours. Yet for the man and the reporter, it seemed only minutes since she had asked her opening question.

Finally she placed her pen on her pad and said, "Remarkable. Do you continue your Partners Meetings?"

"Faithfully. I rarely miss. Some members who've moved away fly back to attend. Others join a meeting in their new hometown or start their own."

"This is incredible. How many of these groups exist?"

"Lots. I honestly don't know the number. They're happening all over the country through the On-Purpose Network."

"Next question: What's happening with the GEOMay contract?"

"We kept the contract. It's been better than any of us imagined. We've even formed a joint venture with GEOMay Company to produce and market a product line called Lamplighter. We've raised our standards to new levels of TOP performance, thanks to that relationship."

"There are just two more questions that remain unanswered, then we can wrap up this interview." Checking the hour from the gold pocket watch on the man's desk, she added, "We've been at this awhile."

"Ask me your question," the man invited.

She flipped through her notebook. "I want to go back to something. Why are you going public about the On-Purpose Business?"

"That's simple. I promised the professor and Bob that I would share what I learned about the On-Purpose Business. I'm not 'going public,' to use your term. I'm simply answering your questions. Perhaps you're the first reporter to pick up on it as newsworthy."

She said, "I must admit, there's a bigger story here than I anticipated."

## THE GOLD WATCH

"And your last question?" he asked.

"The gold watch. Tell me the story of this gold watch."

"Ah, the gold watch," the man commented. "That's what brings all this together. The week after my visit to the Partners Meeting, Mrs. Taylor came by my office. She gave me Fred's gold pocket watch from his retirement party and a personal note penned by him. The watch is symbolic of the message. Fred's note was the clarion call that radically shifted my personal perspective, and ultimately the course of this business. Ironically, Fred's greatest contribution to this company was made after his death."

"How?" urged the reporter as she flipped to a clean sheet of paper.

"Mrs. Taylor said to me, 'My late husband was fond of you. You probably realized it, yet rarely heard it. Fred was stoic and a man whose ways were . . . shall I say, set. He saw it as his strength; yet in the end it was his Waterloo. Holding in his feelings contributed to his stress and heart disease, which ultimately led to his premature death.'

"I said, 'Yes, ma'am, I know Fred cared a great deal about his work, this company, and its people. He didn't openly express it much. His actions spoke loudly, even if he didn't.'

"She thanked me with a warm smile and continued, 'He sacrificed much for the business. Those of us closest to him also paid a high price. His escalating heart problems forced him to face death. Fred was a thorough man;

he prepared for his death. He wanted to reach out to those of you with whom he worked.

"'With his remaining time he sought to make amends. Within our family, many hurts were healed. While he struggled to express himself verbally, he became quite eloquent and free with a pen in hand.'

"I nodded in respect and didn't utter a word. Her eyes teared up, and her voice wavered. She then said, 'We had a good marriage. Fred confided many things to me. Feelings frightened him. He feared not being needed, not being a good leader. He feared change and many other ghosts. As the monthly financial statements went, so did Fred's emotions.

"'He had nowhere and no one to turn to in these times. The complexity of his business problems were beyond my experience and advice. I often wondered how he held up under the pressure. His job was everything to him—it was his identity.'

"'Yes, Mrs. Taylor,' I said. 'Fred was dedicated to this company.' I wasn't sure where she was leading, so I just listened.

"'Dedicated! To a fault!' Mrs. Taylor snapped back. Now more animated, she resumed, 'Did you know these last years as CEO were his worst years? After all those years of climbing the corporate ladder of success, finally reaching the highest rung—and all he found were loneliness, confusion, and frustration. The rapid changes in the marketplace and the demise of the old ways of doing business all contributed to his quiet depression in the midst of external "success."

"'His inability to reach out forced him to go somewhere. He turned inward, in a most negative way. All his emotions shut down except rage. Knowing that he was responsible for the erosion of the company's market leadership was his most devastating realization. It weighed heavily on him. His instincts, honed over forty-eight years, which had served him so well, were now betraying him.

"'The world changed, but Fred clung to the past. As the company spiraled downward, so did Fred's emotional and physical health. He was caught in a web of his own making. His options were played.'

"I said, 'I had no idea Fred was going through so much. If only he had asked for help, certainly . . .'

"'If only!' she abruptly interrupted. 'If only. Oh, how I hate those two little words. In Fred's last days we talked about our life together, our children's lives, and his life and career. Fred kept saying, "If only I had known about this or that." I think my husband came to view his whole life in those two words, "If only . . ." With death looming near, he summoned his remaining strength and decided no more "if only's."'

"I said, 'I'm not sure I understand.'

"'Fred was determined,' she continued, 'to bring positive closure on a life filled with regrets and "if only's." That's my reason for seeing you. You are one of the people he wanted to reach. I am Fred's messenger. His hope is that you'll learn from his life.'"

The reporter said, "This is heavy stuff."

The man responded, "And what a messenger she was. Her face, words, presence, posture, and conviction were angelic. It was as if God was speaking through her to me.

## THE GIFT

"Mrs. Taylor continued, 'May I present my late husband's gift and message for you?'

"She handed me a small, neatly wrapped box and a letter with my name, hand-addressed. I recognized Fred's handwriting.

"Opening the package, I immediately recognized Fred's retirement pocket watch. I thought it was a nice gesture. I pried open the soft gold cover with my thumbnail and read the inscription, 'To Frederick W. Taylor, in honor of forty-eight years of faithful service and leadership.' I was touched that Fred bequeathed his prized watch to me.

"Little did I know what was in store for me in Fred's letter. I read it aloud."

The man opened his desk drawer, pulled out a folder, and began to read to the reporter:

To my friend and business associate,

My days are numbered and my words to you long past due. Even as my physical strength drains, I find a renewed strength and faith in a peace that passes all understanding.

Reflecting on my life, I come to this final passage called death. In the end it is my loving wife and children who are with me. I've sought forgiveness from many and especially them.

It was my damn unavailability. I was so busy building a business that I forgot to build a life. I was too busy for ball games, recitals, birthdays, and just plain hanging around with my family. I realize it isn't as simple as quality time. The key is available time. If I'm not raising my children, then someone else is. Thank goodness for my wife — at least they had one of us. My kids missed out on having a father, and my wife on a husband.

I was a provider, but not a parent or husband.

Make no mistake, a father and husband were preferred to a provider. I remain proud of my lifetime business accomplishments; yet, today they are but hollow achievements from my new vantage point.

It's ironic that a neglected heart is killing me and yet setting me free to be me. Clinically it's called coronary disease. Realistically, it was my dis-ease with life itself—the emptiness inside my heart nearly cost me my wife, my family, the business, and, ultimately, is claiming my life.

Had I exercised my heart physically and emotionally, perhaps I, too, could have had an active and long retirement like a man I know named Hal Trudy. Get to know him. He'll share truths with you that years ago I regrettably rejected as hogwash. I was too skeptical and arrogant to learn. Hal was right! Hal is finishing strong.

The man smiled. "Isn't it amazing! I probably met Hal about the time Fred was composing this letter. He had no idea Hal and I had met." He returned to reading Fred's letter.

So a physical and emotional hardness of heart is the culprit of my condition. What were my options? How might I have done it all differently? If only I had built my life from the inside out instead of from the outside in, I know beyond any reasonable doubt that the health and well-being of my family, the company, and I would be more richly blessed. I did some deals, but I didn't build a business. I leave no legacy.

I accept responsibility for my ill-fated decisions.

My choices led me to this irreversible point of physical decline. My destiny is determined; only the date remains unknown. You are no different than I, except you have more options. You have choices that have not been fully played out to their ultimate conclusion.

That's why I'm bequeathing you my pocket watch. I want it to serve as a constant reminder to learn from my errors before the eleventh hour.

You, like me, are consumed with your career and the success of the business, which are definitely honorable aspirations in the proper perspective. As the Ghost of Christmas Future did for Ebenezer Scrooge in Charles Dickens' *A Christmas Carol*, I hope I, too, am lifting the veil to your future. My path was a dead end. If only you knew what I know now, you would live your life differently. You would find your way home.

Our personal lives are more important than our professional lives. Is that a startling revelation? For me it was! I measured my life by what I did, what I earned, and what job I had. Please don't misunderstand me. Work and a career are important. After all, God put Adam on the earth to work the garden, not to be on some feel-good vacation seven days a week.

The man smiled and commented, "That's vintage Fred." Continuing the letter, he read,

Even Adam in the Garden of Eden needed companionship in addition to God. Sharing life — this is the real wealth of living.

Look at the long-term price of my misplaced priorities. How many men and women of high competence and quality of character did I drive from our company? How many did I burn out in the name of quarterly results? It was a short-term, high-payoff strategy with long-run destructive implications. I failed to offer meaningful work and to foster a sense of community.

You, on the other hand, have a chance to change it. You set the environment as the leader. Don't idly agree that our personal lives are more important than our professional lives; embrace this truth. People watch your actions. Lead by example. Instill this value in the company.

Create a business where personal and professional lives can exist in harmony. Create a community where the business supports the person and family instead of the person and family supporting the business. With my way, the price is too dear. It wasn't even good business.

Great companies come from great people. Great companies cannot make great people. We as leaders play a key role in helping ordinary people accomplish extraordinary results. The rewards accrue to all. We can never rise above the collective personal greatness of the people around us. Work must be more than a paycheck. Tap into the "more," and you tap into people's genius.

It begins with you — the leader of the company. Get straight personally. It's the best thing you can do for the business.

Yes, my gold pocket watch is to be a reminder of my way of life, my successes and my failures. I nearly blew it all! Belatedly, I've been graced with a little time in the waning days of my life to salvage a remnant. I'm taking action now. I don't ever recall being so alive. Ironically, in the midst of dying, death is setting me free. I'm expressing my love to my wife, children, and grandchildren as never before. No more "if only's." The past is the past. No future regrets. No future regrets!

You are my hope and my professional legacy. You can alter the course of events. You can redeem my regrets if you accept my challenge. It begins with you and now it ends with you. Listen to a man with a whole life perspective. Yes, the business matters. No, it is not the source of our true identity and success. At best, it is a place to live out a portion of our purpose in life.

I beseech you to take up this message and turn to a new manner of conducting yourself and the company.

Sincerely yours,
Frederick W. Taylor


The man paused for a long moment, then looked straight at the reporter as he continued his reverie. "Tears welled in my eyes. Mrs. Taylor became a watery blur as Fred's message sank into my being. I said to Mrs. Taylor, 'I'm speechless as to why Fred would reach out to me like this.'

"'That's easy, because the two of you are so alike,' she told me.

"'We are not!' I protested.

"'Oh, yes, you are. Why do you think you became Fred's replacement? The board knew the company was built around a hard-driving skeptic who was committed to nothing else but his career and this company. They replaced Fred with another Fred. Fred told me so himself.

"'You were the only one who fit the job description. The Old Man said, "He's the man. You can't teach him a thing unless you whack him over the head with a stick. When I was his age I was the same way, and look at where it got me.'"

"'I didn't know I was like Fred,' I said.

"'How could you not know?' she replied in disbelief."

The man turned again to the reporter. "Can you believe it? I didn't know that I didn't know. Fred possessed every quality I despised—in myself. It was no wonder I couldn't get him out of my thoughts. We were so much alike. Fred was my mentor whether I realized it or not.

"Rarely does one get to glimpse into a crystal ball. Fred lifted the curtain to the future, and I didn't like what I saw. Some changes in my life were long overdue. The Four Pillars showed me a different path the one Fred and I had been traveling. All I learned about the On-Purpose Business was meaningless, unless I accepted Fred's challenge.

"My spirit was torn and my heart was touched. This was my epiphany, my wake-up call for life. I looked up from Fred's note and said, 'Mrs. Taylor, Fred was a good man. I wouldn't be where I am today had he not cared about me. I accept his challenge to live life differently here at work—and at home.'

"Her face radiated joy. She rose and approached me. I respectfully rose from my chair. Gently placing a hand on each side of my face, she gazed at me as if I were a new-born. In fact, I felt like one who had been washed clean. I had been given a new lease on life. No 'if only's.' She pulled my face toward hers and tenderly kissed my cheek.

"Mrs. Taylor's closing remarks to me were 'Fred was a good man. You now know the man I married and the man I buried. In between, my husband lost himself. Finally, he found his way home. Thank you for answering his lament. God bless you!'

"And with that, she turned and walked out the door."

The reporter sat hushed and wide-eyed. "What did you do next?"

"I sat alone at my desk holding Fred's gold pocket watch and letter. I was dumbfounded. I cradled the pocket watch in my hand for the longest time. I don't know how long I sat there just staring at it and thinking. Finally, I picked up the phone and dialed.

"'Hello,' came my wife's voice.

"I said, 'Hi, honey! I'm coming home early tonight. I want to share a gift for us that Mrs. Taylor brought by from Fred. I've learned some things here at work that will help us. Let's talk about making our lives and marriage on-purpose.'

"'Are you all right?' my wife asked.

"'I'm fine,' I said. 'And another thing: I'm making an appointment to see a man named John Harold. He has something I think I need. Will you please go with me? This is something you've wanted for a long time. Now I do, too. Sorry, honey, I didn't know what you know.'

"'Are you sure you're okay?' she double-checked.

"'Sweetie, I've never been better,' I assured her. Finally, I stopped beating around the bush and said, 'Honey, I love you. I'm coming home.'"

# ABOUT THE AUTHOR

KEVIN MCCARTHY first read the book I'm OK, You're OK, in 1968. This was the start of a personal development process that took him through thousands of hours of reading, contemplating, searching, listening, and discovering. It culminated in *The On-Purpose Person*, his first book. Kevin is a classically educated businessman with an highly entrepreneurial inclination. He graduated from Lehigh University with a bachelor of science degree in business and economics. Graduate business school was the logical step after three years in corporate banking and general management of a business. Kevin received his MBA from The Darden School of the University of Virginia in 1982.

Kevin founded US Partners, Inc. in 1983. He offered his first On-Purpose Business seminar for real estate brokers in 1987. This strategic planning approach was geared to those who needed to plan strategically, yet lacked the time, experience or inclination. The method was simple, "Love your work, know why, and here's how." That seminar became the basis for The On-Purpose Business.

Kevin was born on Christmas Day, 1954 in Pittsburgh, PA. He graduated from Shady Side Academy. Today, he lives in Orlando, FL with his wife, Judith, and their children Charles and Anne. He's active in his church and community. He reads biographies, business and personal development books.

"I'm the steward of a gift called, 'being on-purpose.' I'm in awe seeing this message profoundly touching lives and influencing organizations. It's a privilege I'm compelled to share." Kevin founded The On-Purpose College to train mentors and consultants to help spread the "on-purpose" message.

He is a Professional Member of the National Speakers Association and offers keynote addresses, workshops, and seminars about being on-purpose.

# ON-PURPOSE RESOURCES

Do you want your business or career to become an On-Purpose Business?

US Partners Consulting can help. Our consultants are experienced practitioners with diverse backgrounds and common beliefs in the value of being an on-purpose business.

Contact US Partners Consulting at the address below for a free On-Purpose Business Development Tool to help get your career or organization on-purpose.

THE ON-PURPOSE COLLEGE is dedicated to the development of resources for the training and development of on-purpose persons. Using both *The On-Purpose Person* and *The On-Purpose Business*, the college serves on-purpose persons so they may be on-purpose where they work, volunteer, worship, gather, and live. The College certifies Mentors who are available for personal mentoring and small-group programs.

THE ON-PURPOSE COLLEGE BOOKSTORE offers on-purpose resources such as books, workbooks, tapes, and other items to enhance your efforts of being on-purpose.

Write to either US Partners Consulting or The On-Purpose College at:

PO Box 1568
Winter Park, FL 32790-1568
(407) 657-6000

Please visit our home page on the web at:
www.on-purpose.com